The Total Man

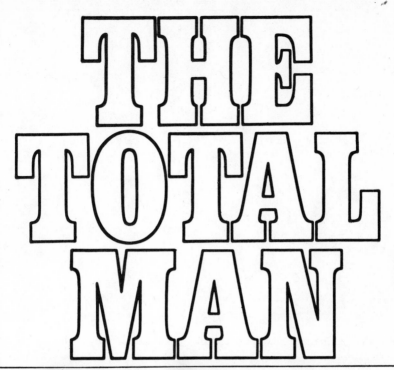

THE TOTAL MAN

Dan Benson

TYNDALE
HOUSE
PUBLISHERS, INC.
WHEATON,
ILLINOIS

Unless otherwise indicated, Bible references are from the New American Standard Bible.

Library of Congress Catalog Card Number 76-58134. ISBN 0-8423-7290-3, paper. Copyright © 1977 Tyndale House Publishers, Inc. Wheaton, Illinois. All rights reserved. Second printing, April 1977. Printed in the United States of America.

CONTENTS

To Kathy,
my wife,
lover,
consultant,
best friend
and partner
in life's greatest
adventure:
that of becoming
balanced,
fulfilled,
total persons.

It was two years ago now as I was browsing through a bookstore. There, as I scanned the "Marriage and Family" shelves, the flame ignited inside me.

Something was wrong. Something was missing. I saw *How to Satisfy Your Man, The Total Woman, Fascinating Womanhood, You Can Be the Wife of a Happy Husband,* and scores of other feminine titles. Judging from the books that had been written and read, it appeared that the *woman* was the only spouse responsible for a successful marriage and happy family.

Where did the man fit in? Well, he was over on aisle seven—under "Success," "Business Management," and "Money-making Opportunities." *His* books told him how to become the next instant millionaire, how to rise in the business world, how to think positively toward a higher tax bracket. Something was definitely wrong. And the flame within me began to burn brighter, hotter.

INTRODUCTION

For several years I'd been watching an odd phenomenon. I saw men, some of them close friends, pouring their lives into their careers. Working ten, twelve hours a day. Traveling thousands of miles each year. Sitting through hours of important committee meetings. Getting reports, files, and proposals in before deadline.

My friends were rising fast, doing "meaningful" work, getting bigger salaries and better benefits. But I could see that deep down inside, a restless feeling gnawed at their bellies.

And if they were married, the restlessness was even more evident. Left behind, at home, were the beautiful wife and children. Too bad work was so demanding. "Honey, I'm late ... can we talk about this some other time?" "Not now, Son, I'm busy—how about Sunday?" But for some reason, "some other time" and "Sunday" rarely came. I watched helplessly as husband and wife, father and child, slowly grew worlds apart.

On that day in the bookstore, I knew that things had to change. They *must*. It was past time for a book for *men* which would help them find that important balance between personal fulfillment, career, and family life. It was past time for a *man's* book which went beyond theory, beyond preaching, to explore hundreds of very practical ways in which today's man can be a smashing success at home as well as on the job.

Today, two years later, the flame burns even brighter within me, but it has changed from one of despair to one of excitement. For I know that I've said what needs to be said. I'm convinced that the message of the following pages is what we men have needed to hear, comprehend, and act upon for decades. And I'm excited at what we are about to discover together as we sit down and talk man to man, heart to heart.

We're going to explore, and explode, a few myths about manhood. We'll examine the need for a better balance between our personal lives, family lives, and careers. And most important, we're going to come upon some very practical and *fun* ways to establish and maintain that crucial balance.

My sincere thanks goes to several friends who have shared the burning flame with me. Mom and Dad, Dale and Barb, Jay and Vicky, and Paul and Barb—all of the Benson clan; and Mom and Dad and Dennis and Elma—of the Means family—sent many good suggestions my way and many prayers heavenward. Lowell and Pam Heim, my close friends and a super-successful couple in their own right, invested several hours with me in creative brainstorming and constructive criticism. Carolyn Jones's typing—often on very short notice—was always cheerful and superb.

At Tyndale House, I owe a big debt of gratitude to Vic Oliver, who gave me both go-ahead and guidance on the manuscript, and to his staff, whose expert editing helped turn a few of my more outspoken thoughts into softspoken ones.

But most of all: Kathy Benson, you sweet little charmer of a wife, I thank you publicly, for all the world to see. For your love, confidence, and encouragement were just as strong when the words weren't flowing as when they were. Come here, Love. The book's completed. The message is out. Let's go celebrate.

Dan Benson, Colorado Springs

Section
One

THE LIBERATED MAN

1 Free to Be a Man

Man, n. An animal so lost in rapturous contemplation of what he thinks he is as to overlook what he indubitably ought to be.

AMBROSE BIERCE

It was a perceptive ad agency that conceived the "Marlboro Man."

There he stands, long and lean, rugged and free. The sun glints off the ruddy crags in his face. Behind him, a herd of galloping mustangs symbolize his strength, daring, and hard-tack masculinity.

Those who created him knew that he would portray America's masculine dream—our subconscious symbol of the brooding, rugged independence that spells *maleness*. Whether we indulge in his tubular product or not, his life-style sums up what we strive for: Freedom. Success. The ability to handle any situation that comes along. The strong, silent disposition that expresses nothing short of total manhood.

Men, sit down. Look around.

The American masculine dream is killing us.

For years we have been taught that a man must be an unswerving pinnacle of strength. Emotion and gentleness were for sissies. At school it was manly to play football, unmanly to cry. At home it was masculine to chop wood or repair the car; unmasculine to help with the dishes or housework. At the office it is manly to exercise cold shrewdness for the sake of the profit margin, unmanly to show sensitivity and caring for the problems of a fellow-worker.

In short, we have subscribed to what the Spanish call *machismo,* the concept that our masculinity is proportionate to how well we wear our strong, silent toughness. In modern times the word has been shortened to *macho.*

Says Jack O. Balswick, professor of sociology at the University of Georgia, "In learning to be a man, the boy in America comes to value indications of masculinity expressed largely through physical courage, toughness, competitiveness, and progressiveness. Femininity is, in contrast, expressed largely through gentleness and responsiveness. Parents teach their sons that a real man does not show his emotions."

The result?

Whenever you have the opportunity, observe the aged. In the vast majority of elderly married couples, you'll find one of the following to be true: (1) The husband has passed away, survived several years by his wife, or (2) if both are still living but one is infirm, it is often the husband. The one-time tower of strength is now pampered, wheeled about, and spoon-fed by his still-healthy wife.

He is the victim of an unspoken societal code which dictates that it is not masculine for a man to cry, to seek help, to express tenderness, or otherwise release pent-up emotions. So over the years the guilt, fears, and frustrations wear his body and mind down to a frazzle. He seeks escape in illnesses more often psychosomatic than organic. And in the end, the man's physical and emotional life is drained, affecting his wife, family, relationships, job—everything upon which he has built his life. Is that surprising, when we take a look at the expected American life-style, whose furious pace surpasses that of almost every other nation?

Time magazine recently reported that "American men have one of the highest heart disease rates in the world; 378 out of every 100,000 die as a result of coronary attacks each year." The article cites a study by researchers at the University of California at Berkeley, who concluded that "stress, American style, is a major cause of coronaries."

The team studied the life-styles of 4,000 Japanese men (who have one of the world's *lowest* heart disease rates), delving into their "diets, cholesterol levels, smoking habits, and other factors usually associated with heart disease. When the data were finally analyzed, it became apparent that the Japanese who cling to their traditional life-styles, which defuse tension by emphasizing acceptance of the individual's place in both family and society, fare well.... But those who adopt the aggressive, competitive, and impatient traits of most Americans increasingly succumb to the strain.... Those who plunged most fully into the stress of American life were five times as likely to have coronaries as those who maintained Japanese ways."

We're suffering, men, from a widespread epidemic of pseudo-masculinity.

Macho.

It has placed our entire existence on a performance basis, our manhood's "success" or "failure" being determined more by *what we do* than by *who we are*. It is eroding our physical, mental, emotional, and spiritual health. And, by dictating those long, hard hours and strong, silent dispositions, it has created massive love-and-communication gaps between us and our families.

Do you see it happening? In striving to be like the Marlboro Man, we've become more imprisoned than free.

That's why we're in urgent need of liberation.

Liberation. The word scares a lot of people. And if I've learned anything from the feminist movement, it's that you've got to clearly define your terms. Women's "lib" to one means an all-out, no-holds-barred freedom from all home responsibilities. To another, it's equality in jobs and roles. A third person sees it as equality in personhood with a differ-

entiation in roles. To a fourth, it may merely mean the free
dom to go with or without a bra. "Liberation" sparks controversy, especially if it isn't defined prior to discussion.

So when I speak of "men's liberation," I want my readers
to make no mistake about my definition.

Men's liberation is the resolute, unabashed freedom *from*
society's false standards of masculinity, *to* a more relaxed,
confident manhood. It's based on the simple fact that you
don't have to *prove* your manhood—you *are* a man! It frees
you:

—to express love, gentleness, and kindness
—to slow down and relax
—to value your wife and family as more important than
  your job
—to show emotion—even cry—if you need to
—to take time to be healthy
—to better fulfill your wife emotionally and sexually
—to give more attention to your highest priorities in life
—to *enjoy* life to the maximum
—to say "no" to the activities which have been draining
  your time and energy
—to possess your money wisely, without being possessed
  by it
—to pursue a different brand of success

...and not feel the slightest bit threatened as a man. Because
deep down, you'll be discovering a dimension of maleness
more fulfilling than a thousand great American success
stories. You'll discover the freedom to be the man, husband,
and father you've always wanted to be.

You'll discover the total man.

2 Your Tower of Success

What has happened

—when H. G. Wells, after achieving world fame as a writer and historian, writes: "I have no peace. All life is at the end of the tether"?

—when Samuel T., now vice president of his firm and due for another salary hike next May, suddenly realizes that his children have no respect for him?

—when Howard Hughes, after becoming one of the world's wealthiest tycoons, holes himself up in eccentric seclusion for years and finally dies of malnutrition?

—when a well-known U.S. senator, after his meteoric rise to the top, is divorced by his wife who says "our marriage just simply died"?

—when Michael W., after spending seventy hours a week getting his own "dream" business going, is suddenly flattened by a heart attack and confined to a hospital bed?

—when Ralph Barton, once one of the nation's foremost cartoonists, leaves this

19

note as he takes his life: "I have had few difficulties, many friends, great successes; I have gone from wife to wife and from house to house, visited great countries of the world, but I am fed up with inventing devices to fill up twenty-four hours of the day"?

—when Ernest Hemingway, the leading writer of his day and still one of history's most "successful," is haunted by paranoia until he blasts his head apart with a shotgun?

What's happened?

All of these men were at, or near, the top of their chosen professions. Goal-reachers. They knew no lack of money, reputation, or power. They all had found what we've come to call success.

Then why all the desperation?

One look at these men, and then another look at the thousands around us who are similarly striving, brings to a head another concept from which we are in urgent need of liberation: the American idea of success. It has probably caused more disenchantments, marital problems, generation gaps, and ulcers than the most prolific soap opera writer could dream of.

Now I'm not saying for a moment that success is wrong. That's like saying that sex and money are wrong, and I personally need all three. Our culprit is a wrong *concept* of success. It has crammed us into a mold that not only thwarts the individual potential each of us has, but runs us ragged in the process of chasing it.

Real success should be a value in life which signifies that we are *living and growing to maximum potential as persons.* It should call each of us to a fulfilling interplay of our mental, physical, spiritual, and social dimensions—to "Be all we can be."

But we Americans are an impatient, result-oriented people. We can't see or measure a value, much less hang it in the trophy room. So, like each of the successful failures mentioned above, we have pinned this value onto something tangible—a bank account, a car, a house, a position, a statistical goal (even some very worthy ones). And in obtaining these tangibles, we hope to experience enough euphoria to justify calling them "success."

In *The American Idea of Success,* Richard Huber confirms this observation:

> In America, success has meant making money and translating it into status, or becoming famous.... Success was not earned by being a loyal friend or good husband. It was a reward for performance on the job.... Success was not simply *being* rich or famous. It meant *attaining* riches or *achieving* fame.

The result is a distorted, performance-oriented creed which holds that our manhood is proportionate to our earning power.

The other day I overheard one woman telling another that it was "hard on Joe's manhood" that he didn't get the promotion he was bucking for. My question is: What does Joe's promotion have to do with his manhood?

Absolutely nothing!

What's gone wrong with our thinking? Basically, a confusion between our *needs* and *desires.* To illustrate this important concept, let's construct a "tower" of building blocks to represent the successful man.

At the foundation must go our *Fulfillment Needs*—those basic, nonoptional aspects of life which will account for our personal fulfillment. The foundation of the total man's tower of life will consist of four building blocks representing the four basic dimensions of his personality: the physical, mental, social, and spiritual. Only by meeting these Fulfillment Needs can one find that inner peace psychologists call "self-actualization"—realizing that you are becoming a maximum person.

But why is it that so many people don't realize their Fulfillment Needs? Because they have wrongly identified what those needs are. Because this foundation is so crucial to a fulfilling life-style, we'll come back and examine it more closely in a moment.

THE TOTAL MAN

On top of our foundation we'll place our *Survival Needs*—food, shelter, clothing, job, finances, recreation, and so on. All of these are vital to our existence, and in proper amounts serve to complement the processing of our Fulfillment Needs.

Then, least vital of the three but still desirable, are our *Wants and Desires*—a better house, a higher income, a stereo system, a sports car, etc. Call them the icing of life—not fully necessary, but capable of enhancing our fulfillment and survival.

The properly constructed tower will look like this:

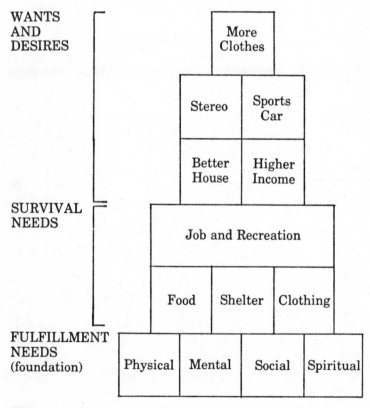

Perhaps now you're beginning to see what happened to the men listed at the start of this chapter. Each had somehow let his *Wants and Desires* take priority over his Fulfillment Needs. It's a common mistake. Much too common. We like to see life in measurable terms, and since man is difficult to measure, we watch the stat sheet instead. It's much easier to answer a question like "How much did I make in my lifetime?" than "What kind of a man am I?"

The "tower" such men build might look like this:

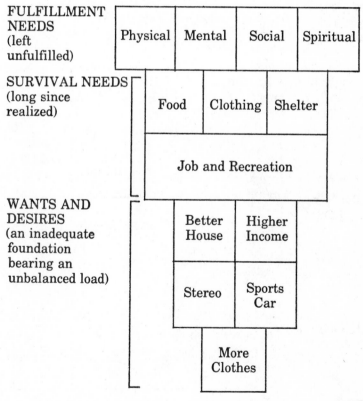

FULFILLMENT NEEDS (left unfulfilled)

| Physical | Mental | Social | Spiritual |

SURVIVAL NEEDS (long since realized)

| Food | Clothing | Shelter |

Job and Recreation

WANTS AND DESIRES (an inadequate foundation bearing an unbalanced load)

| Better House | Higher Income |
| Stereo | Sports Car |

More Clothes

THE TOTAL MAN

But once those men had achieved their *Wants and Desires* (they had long since met their *Survival Needs*), that question began to haunt them. "What kind of a man am I?" They could no longer rely on statistics. They finally realized that they were unfulfilled as persons. All along, life had held something deeper, but they had been blind to it.

They had each gone about life upside-down, going after the *least* important things to the near exclusion of the *most* important. Their foundation, inverted and made of the wrong material, could not possibly bear the burden of all the other facets of life. It could only crumble.

And now let's get personal. If we were to build a tower representing *your* life, how would it stand today?

You've probably come to the conclusion by now that the key to a life of genuine success lies in the *foundation. Whatever* you have placed there is your standard of success.

Is your personal foundation strong enough? Below is a little quiz to help you determine what criteria for success you've been following:

1. Ask yourself: "If I were suddenly stripped of all money (and the ability to earn it), all position (and the ability to gain it), and all the statistical goals I have been striving for, what would be left of me to make me a 'successful' man?"

2. Study this list of aspects of a man's life—all the goals, events, and things which make up a normal day. You may be able to think of more—if so, write them in.

  _____ house
  _____ finances
  _____ car(s)
  _____ friendships
  _____ job
  _____ hobbies
  _____ relationship with wife
  _____ relationship with children
  _____ higher position, better salary
  _____ physical health
  _____ food

_____ mental development
_____ reading
_____ golf, tennis, other sports
_____ spiritual fulfillment
_____ camping
_____ stereo system
_____ furnishings
_____ reaching a goal
_____ education
_____ TV programs
_____ clothes

_____ _____
_____ _____
_____ _____

Now be honest—no one is looking but you. Place a check-mark beside the item(s) that have commanded the most attention from you during the past two or three months.

Of course there will be exceptions, but it's reasonable to assume that those items which you've checked make up your criteria for success, or your foundation. At least, you've been pursuing them as if they do.

3. Now answer the telling question: "Do the items I've checked indicate that I want to be a success as a person, or be a success merely in having and doing things?"

I've purposely delayed elaborating on what goes into the successful foundation so that you would first have opportunity to evaluate your own. If you didn't fare so well, don't worry. The important thing is to have an open mind and heart, and a thirst for a more genuine, worthwhile brand of success.

If you do, read on. You're on the road to a refreshing new perspective on life.

R

3 The Solid Foundation

Some men succeed by what they know; some by what they do; and a few by what they are.
ELBERT HUBBARD

It's obvious that the popular definition of success is leaving many of us unsatisfied.

Some of us are tense and miserable because we've been unable to reach our own standards. Inflation, unemployment, a missed promotion, an emergency, or even "bad luck" have prevented many of us from attaining that good life we've set sights on.

Others of us survive those lumps and actually reach our goals. For a while, there's a certain happy feeling. Life may become a little easier with the added money, better clothing, and nicer homes that success has brought us. But what then?

As John Peterson wrote in the *National Observer,* "The home in suburbia, the cars and televisions, the children, the weekends around the barbecue or behind the power mower" [are enjoyed by more than half of all Americans today, but] *"surveys show that two-thirds of them would like to change their lives significantly.*

27

"The good life, it turns out, not only isn't enough; at times it seems hardly palatable" (italics mine).

In calling for men's liberation, I'm convinced it's past time we stripped success of its artificial trappings. Obviously our current definition isn't bringing happiness. If something doesn't work, let's get rid of it and find something that *does!*

It's time for us to take success out of the realm of what we *earn, have,* or *do.* Sure these are nice, but they're not enough. It's time to place success in a more meaningful realm: what kind of men we *are.*

Are. That doesn't mean accumulating money or things, or even doing great deeds. We don't *have* to climb any corporate ladders or hold positions on committees. No bank accounts, stock reports, Cadillacs, or *Who's Who* writeups are necessary.

All that's necessary is you, developing the personality God gave you to become a complete man!

And that's where your *Fulfillment Needs* come in.

The solid foundation—your virtual guarantee of fulfilled manhood—is a four-block foundation that focuses on *being* before having or doing. Each block (a *fulfillment need)* depends on the other three for maximum strength, requiring a balanced emphasis upon each of the four. We find this four-fold foundation in the developing manhood of Jesus Christ:

> And Jesus kept increasing in wisdom and stature, and in favor with God and men (Luke 2:52).

```
┌─────────────┐
│             │
│  WISDOM     │
│             │
└─────────────┘
```

Wisdom. A study of the life of Christ indicates that he was no slouch when it came to a knowledge of current events, politics, and nature. He understood the Scriptures more thoroughly than the most "religious" people of his day. But it was his uncanny ability to weave all this knowledge into a meaningful life-style that made him truly wise. Christ was a thinking man, making practical what others knew as mere theory.

WISDOM	STATURE

Stature. Can you imagine what thirty years' work in a carpenter shop would do for the back and shoulder muscles? We aren't told much about Christ's appearance, but the indirect evidence is enough to convince me that I wouldn't want to face him in a football game.

—He could walk miles of deserts, from one town to the next, and still have energy to meet people's needs.

—Twice he took a bullwhip and singlehandedly drove mobs of hucksters out of the temple.

—His voice was powerful enough to be heard by more than 5,000 people at once—outdoors.

—He had a physical charisma which prompted people to drop what they were doing and join him when he said, "Follow me."

—He took care of his body. Several times we see him "getting away" to rest and refresh himself with prayer and sleep. He knew when rejuvenation was more important than work.

WISDOM	STATURE	FAVOR WITH GOD

Favor with God. The fact that Christ was God's Son didn't give him any special "in." Christ's mission on earth was twofold: 1) To die as the last sacrifice ever needed for our sin, thus making it possible for us to have intimate fellowship with God, and 2) to perfectly exemplify total manhood for us, without the aid of his divine attributes. In other words, he temporarily laid aside his powers as God to show us what a total man can be!

But as a man, a total man, he knew that man is not only a mental and physical creature, but a *spiritual* being as well.

As a result, Christ spent much time in private conversation with God, considering God a partner in everything he did. Then, like today, all kinds of phony "spiritual experiences" clamored for his attention. But Christ set his eyes on the only true God to satisfy his spiritual dimension.

WISDOM	STATURE	FAVOR WITH GOD	FAVOR WITH MAN

Favor with man. Christ was a *social* being who interacted well with people because he genuinely loved them. But he wasn't interested in winning any popularity contests (he upset the establishment on more than one occasion). People either hated him or loved him. Hated, because his integrity couldn't be bought by the insecure Jewish leadership. Loved, because for all his leadership and wisdom, he held the attitude of a *servant*. Meeting the needs of others was his greatest joy.

Christ spent most of his time, however, with an intimate group known as his disciples—loving them and teaching them the vital things they would need to know in life. We could compare them with the *family unit* of today. And here's where his example might shake a few of us up: Though secure in his maleness and strong in his leadership, Christ demonstrated his servant role best *among those with whom he lived.*

Why do these four foundation blocks make up the liberated man's definition of success? *Because they transcend the inadequate, superficial definition of society.* By the world's standards, Jesus Christ was a total failure. He didn't own much, had only enough money to survive, dressed simply.

His most elaborate transportation was a donkey. Of his best friends, one betrayed him and another denied knowing him.

And then—dead at the age of thirty-three, condemned, beaten, stripped, and crucified before a vicious mob of his contemporaries.

A miserable failure—or so the world thought. Three days later, upon his resurrection from the grave, his purpose became clear. He stands today a living example of total, fulfilled personhood. He gives men living proof that eternal, abundant living is theirs for the asking.

What a foundation! Christ's definition of success would not allow society to dictate his standards. He was his own man, completely at peace with himself, because his life was in perfect balance mentally, physically, spiritually, and socially.

It is only on such a foundation that we will meet our needs of personal fulfillment and totality. As those crucial needs are met, then our *Survival Needs* and our *Wants and Desires* will fall into proper perspective. But our main goal in life— our standard of success—must be nothing less than the balanced personal life.

Men, the world's success system is not working. Isn't it time we chucked it for a system that *does?*

How many of us are so busy with our jobs and causes that we haven't learned how to *live?* Do we *really* have a close relationship with our wives and children, or have we allowed work to preempt our home life? Has the stress of "making it" kept us energetic and fit, or has it turned us into mounds of jiggling Jello? How long has it been since we've read a good, mind-stimulating book (and *applied* it to our lives)? And is God just a cosmic force in the sky, or is he a vital, intimate part of our daily routine?

We've been chasing after sirens when the key to maximum success in manhood is right under our noses. I know, because I'm a siren-chaser from way back—and I'm still tempted occasionally to launch out after the tangibles. But I can testify wholeheartedly that God's formula for success works. It has enriched my perspective on life, my love for Kathy, my self-image, my love for others—and it hasn't done a bit of harm toward the attainment of my wants and desires, either.

That's the reason for *The Total Man.* I want you to experience the joy of knowing that you are becoming all you can be—that you will be able at any point in life to say without reservation, "I am a success!" I want you to experience a renewed intimacy of love, communication, and togetherness with your wife and children—and the happy home that results. I want you to be free from society's false concept that manhood is based on performance—*free to assert your manhood on the basis of character.*

Success is what you *are!*

Are you with me? Then come along. Let's explore some essential, practical ways to strengthen that foundation.

4 Three Keys to Liberation from the Clock

Half our life is spent trying to find something to do with the time we have rushed through life trying to save.
WILL ROGERS

One concept we need to shake loose from right now is the idea that hurrying leads to greatness.

A century ago, if a westward traveler happened to miss the Wells Fargo stagecoach, he wasn't concerned. After all, another stage would be coming through again next week. But today it's a different story: We'll panic if we miss one section of a revolving door.

We live in a culture whose pace intensifies in direct proportion to its technology and its profit motive. That's getting pretty fast. No longer is it enough just to work hard. To "redeem the time" means to work harder and longer, to try to squeeze every possible dollar or result out of the minutes we've been allotted.

In the process, we have assigned ourselves some amazing virtues. The virtue of the bulging briefcase carried home in the evening. The virtue of continually flying from one end of the country to the other on business. The virtue of serving

33

on committees. The virtue of a messy desk. The virtue of the hasty peck-on-the-cheek for the wife. The virtue of late evenings, and nights, at the office. The virtue of saying, in all honesty, "I don't have time."

There has come to be great virtue, and distinctive manhood, in the rush. It signifies that our lives are filled with importance and urgency. We are working on something Big. We are *responsible*. If we aren't hurrying, we are therefore lazy.

You'd think that America was short-changed when God handed out the hours in the day. Travel outside our country and you'll be amazed—probably frustrated—by other nations' seeming disregard of the clock. Punctuality and hurrying just aren't that important to them. Some Asian countries, for example, practice what they call "the rubberized hour"—a time of rest or break from routine which can stretch beyond its designated time limit if the person feels the need. It is a time of flexibility, of the gathering-of-wits for the rest of the day. It's frustrating to us, but healthy and invigorating to them. We often regard as wasteful what in reality might be quite wise.

Overwork is simply another manifestation of the *macho* man. Clarence Randall, the former chairman of Inland Steel, refers to it as "the myth of the overworked executive." Randall says, "Such a person is overworked because he wants to be. And frequently, the longer and harder he works, the less effective he becomes.... Pity him, but recognize him for the dangerous liability that he is."

Contrast the overworked man of today with the life of Jesus Christ, and you'll find some startling differences. Christ accomplished his total purpose in just three years of public ministry. He met the physical and spiritual needs of people, confronted the hypocrisy of the religious leaders, disseminated a gospel of spiritual truth which was to change the lives of millions, and trained a group of eleven unlikely men to carry on after he had left them—and even though he

34

knew he had only three years, Christ was never panicked for the lack of time.

His pace was steady and progressive, yet never harried. He often withdrew by himself or with his "family" of disciples for rest and rejuvenation. Yet, at the end of that three-year span, he could look up to his heavenly Father in all confidence and say, "I have glorified you on the earth, having accomplished the work you gave me to do."

So what's *our* hurry?

Christ was living proof that *God has given us all the time we need to accomplish all he has called us to accomplish.* If he has given you a talent with business, he has also provided sufficient time for you to be the best businessman possible—without the frenetic pace. If you are a husband and father, you have plenty of time to do your task at the office and still be a successful husband and parent.

To "redeem the time" does not mean to work longer and harder—that is simply diluting quality with quantity. To "redeem the time" is to invest it wisely to best serve *you.* You can either let time free you, or you can let it beat you to death.

Aren't you about ready—
—to be free from the clock, from the harried pace that could wear you to a frazzle (if it hasn't done so already)?
—to make and follow your own schedule, instead of someone else's?
—to have more time with your wife and children?
—to unclutter your life from the myriad tasks and responsibilities which have been piling up?
—to get the most important things done without being hampered by the trifles?

You can start right now. I'm going to share three keys which will prove invaluable to you the rest of your life. If you'll invest a few moments now to study them and put them to work, you'll be amazed at how soon daylight begins to appear in your schedule.

KEY ONE
Recognize the activities which have been monopolizing your time.

Sit down and make a list of those items which have been consuming too much of your time in recent weeks. Among the most common time monopolizers:

The organization. This is not the Mafia, although sometimes it makes off like a thief with your time and energy. This is the company or cause you are working for.

How much time beyond those eight or nine daily hours is really necessary? Of course, an occasional rush job may keep you late, but some companies seem to specialize in rush jobs. If your work has been usurping your evenings and weekends lately, it's time for you to put your foot down. No matter how "urgent" or "worthy" the task, such a schedule is poison to the healthy, balanced life.

Haste. It's ironic, but it seems that almost every time I hurry, I lose time in the process.

I was fresh out of college and driving toward a town forty-five miles away for my first job interview. Soon I realized that I had underestimated the amount of time the drive would take. Traffic was heavy, and the cars in front of me were moving so slowly that I began to get edgy.

On the outskirts of one town, I spotted an opening and gunned my car around the slow-moving ones. Within minutes, I saw red flashing in my rear-view mirror.

"You crossed a double yellow line back there," the policeman said. "And you were ten miles over the limit when you did it."

Did you know that ticket-writing takes *fifteen minutes?*

I called my prospective employer and told him I would be a little late. "The traffic is pretty heavy today," I told him. I wasn't about to give him the *real* reason. Rushing that way was just plain stupid. Twenty-five dollars' worth of stupid.

36

LIBERATION FROM THE CLOCK

I keep learning that lesson over and over. On the job, I perform better when I work slowly and steadily. When I work on the car, those bolts never want to loosen when I'm in a big rush. A worthwhile question: "How come I never have time to do it right but always have time to do it over?"

The inability to say "No." Either to the organization or to the host of committees, projects, or causes that clamor for your attention.

A newlywed neighbor of ours works as a representative for a worldwide service organization. Out of his first three months of marriage, our friend was away from his wife for *two months.* It isn't that he wanted to travel that much. His supervisors convinced him that the cause he works for deserved the sacrifice.

It's flattering to have people ask us to help with this project or serve on that committee, but many of us are getting flattered to death. We become the "dumping ground" for a bunch of responsibilities other people don't want. We need to establish a firm set of priorities to help us say "Yes" to the best and "No" to the rest.

Television. There's nothing like a football game or a John Denver special to relax me when I've had a full day, but I'll be the first to admit that I'm a potential TV-holic. I'm fully capable of staring at the tube from the 6 o'clock report till the 11 o'clock news. That's *five hours.* For all of its ludicrous programming and weak plots, the TV is a spellbinder which, after a short while, deadens my mind and promotes continuing laziness.

Recognizing my weakness, I *must* try to plan ahead—creative things Kathy and I can do together, projects I've been wanting to begin, good books to read. I don't want to be guilty of devoting five hours of my time each day to that Cyclopean box.

Personal mismanagement. The disorganized flitting from one project to another, or spending too much time on secondary priorities. The most common sign of time mismanagement is the cry, "I've just got too many things to do!" A perceptive man named La Bruyers once wrote, "Those who make the worst use of their time are the first to complain of its brevity." The wise man will not take on so many things in the first place, and if perchance he has just started to become wise, he will proceed to accomplish each item in an orderly, not frenzied, fashion.

Worry and daydreaming. How often do you have to snap yourself from a lengthy daydream or worry session, only to find that time has not waited around for you?

Daydreams can be either constructive or wasteful. Constructive daydreams can spawn fresh, imaginative new ideas—a new invention, a book that needs to be written, creative family nights, a song, or even a new insight into yourself. Wasteful daydreams, on the other hand, take on a negative, escapist tone. They moan "I wish," while constructive daydreams ask "Why not?" With this in mind, you'll know the next time you daydream whether you're killing time or investing it.

Worry is *never* constructive, and for all the harm it causes you'd wonder why it has become one of our favorite pastimes. Worry is usually the result of a mismanagement of our priorities, our time, or our finances. A better use of that worry time would be to rectify our mismanagement than to fret about the circumstances.

Meetings. Is this one really necessary? Is it for routine information that a memo or phone call could handle? In light of the committee's preparation, will it be a pooling of ignorance or a catalyst for ideas?

Stacks of papers. R. Alec MacKenzie, a leading time-management consultant, points out that in any kind of desk or paper work, our tendency is to say, "Look at all those papers. They show how indispensable I am."

In a *U. S. News and World Report* interview, MacKenzie relates this insight from one of his clients:

"Do you know why we stack our desks? It's all those papers we consider so important we don't want to forget them. We leave them right on top where we can see them. Soon our desks become covered with all those important things we don't want to forget. Then, whenever our gaze wanders from the work we are doing, it is arrested by those things we didn't want to forget. So we are interrupted and distracted all day long by our own stacked desks!"

Keep your desk clear of all jobs and papers that don't relate to the present task. You might keep a special table nearby (out of your line of vision) to organize these papers until you're ready for them. By allowing just one job on your desk at a time, your concentration will multiply—and the present task itself will seem much simpler than before. Said Publius Syrus, a first-century B. C. sage, "To do two things at once is to do neither."

Telephone. It's strange that our society has conditioned itself to drop everything and "snap-to" at the mere ring of the telephone. True, there are genuine emergencies and times when friends-in-need take precedence over something I may be doing, but that same telephone can also be a tyrant. Our telephone has interrupted more relaxing evenings, candlelight dinners, lovemaking, counseling sessions, times of family Bible study and prayer ... but that was before I learned to take it off the hook.

Howard Ball, a good friend of mine and president of a consulting services organization for churches, says it's ironic how we feel we must leave the house in order to obtain privacy from the telephone. "It's *my* house, and I am in charge there—not the telephone," Howard says. For those special times of togetherness with his wife and children, he has had the phone company install switches which have a decided advantage over taking the phone off the hook: For the caller, the phone rings; for him, however, the bell doesn't sound.

Now Howard is not antisocial—in fact, he's one of the most warm-hearted, neighborly men I've had the privilege to know. He just knows when to put his personal relaxation and family times before the demands the telephone might make.

Well, these are a few of the most typical time-stealers today, and you've probably thought of some others that have been bugging you. Now that you've identified them, they'll have a harder time sneaking in unnoticed.

KEY TWO
Resolve right now
to slow down
a little.

The Associated Press recently carried this report about men caught up in the hectic pace:

"The final report of an 8½-year study confirms earlier findings that the aggressive, hard-driving individual is much more likely to have a heart attack than a relaxed person.... The study, recently reported in the *Journal of the American Medical Association,* found that men falling into the behavior pattern marked by 'enhanced aggressiveness, ambitiousness, competitive drive and chronic sense of time urgency' had heart attacks more than twice as frequently as those individuals characterized as more relaxed."

You'll be doing yourself and those you love a big favor if you begin right now to slow down a bit. You may be setting a precedent among the men you work with, but it won't take long for them to notice some healthy side effects.

For one thing, they will be calmer because you are calm. Your work will take on a noticeable improvement in quality. You'll begin to notice and really care for people. And best of all, you will have a new appreciation for the beauty and purpose God has created in the world around you—because you are daring to stop and discover.

Have you ever wondered why time seems to go so fast for us as adults? When we were children, it seemed that time just wouldn't move fast enough. The days were long, and the weeks and months seemed to creep by *so* slowly. We couldn't wait to be grown-ups.

But how often we covet all that time (and energy) we had in childhood! Where did all the time go? Why are the days, months, and years spinning by us too quickly?

Routine. We have allowed the clock to bind us into a schedule so regular and hectic that we feel guilty if we pause to reflect, relax, listen, and learn. Thomas Mann and George Gissing are two men who slowed down long enough to notice this very thing:

"When one day is like all the others," writes Mann, "then they are all like one; complete uniformity would make the longest life seem short, and as though it has stolen away from us unawares."

Gissing says, "It is familiarity with life that makes time speed quickly. When every day is a step in the unknown, as for children, the days are long with gathering of experience."

So slow down a bit. Take the time to try some new things. Open up all the senses God gave you to discover life to its fullest. You'll find it a rejuvenating experience.

Now if you're like me, "Slow Down" will take some constant repeating for awhile. Whenever you get that frustrated feeling that circumstances are controlling you, stop. Close your eyes and ask yourself three important questions:

1. "Is it really necessary for me to rush like this?"
2. "What is my present pace doing to me, to my family, to my relationship with God, and to my fellow-workers?"
3. "Is this project worth that?"

If your present pace is causing you to miss out on the balanced life, then you can be sure God is not pleased with your efforts, no matter how noble. He is much more interested in your *being* than he is in your *doing*. And there is no virtue in a frenzied, unbalanced life-style.

KEY THREE
Follow these steps
to make the best
of your time.

Is there a long list of "things to do" hounding at you?

Remember: God has provided all the time you need to

accomplish the tasks he wants you to accomplish. So if you don't have enough time, you have either misused it, or you have taken on responsibilities God never intended you to have.

1. Think out your priorities in life.
What is most important to you in life?

If you are striving to live the balanced life, then your job or your membership on the Worthy Cause Committee will never take precedence over your physical and mental health or your relationships with God and your family. If these are all doing nicely, then a little extra time on the job or committee won't hurt. But if any of these foundational areas may be slighted, it's time to say "No" to the extras.

A wise friend of mine, no loafer in the business world, once confided to me the order of priorities he follows:

> "First, my relationship with God
> Second, my relationship with my wife
> Third, my relationship with my children
> Fourth, my personal development
> Fifth, my business."

I have seen by the joy in his smile, by the unity among his wife and children, by his vibrant health, and by his success in business that such a list of priorities *works*.

2. Make a list of all the things that need to be done.
The big things, the little things. What's on your mind? Don't leave anything out.

3. Eliminate all nonpriority items.
This step is especially important if you have become "swamped" with tasks and responsibilities. Take your list of things to do, and for each item ask, "In light of my life's

priorities, is this task really that important right now?" Will your working on it mean putting off a higher priority for awhile? Then chances are good that you will want to eliminate this lower priority from your list.

Sometimes this step involves a very humbling but necessary procedure: backing out gracefully. More than once in my life I've made the mistake of taking on too much for myself. The problem is that I like people, and when they ask me to serve on a committee, write a promotional piece, or help in some other way, I'm honored. Saying "No" is difficult for me. So, after two or three consecutive months of saying, "Sure, I'd be glad to," reality strikes hard: I'm swamped. I'm doing so many things that I can't give any of them my best shot. And it all causes me to be one unbalanced, pooped-out individual.

First, I have to admit my mistake to myself: I haven't considered my priorities in accepting assignments and responsibilities. Then comes the hard part—going to those who asked me to serve, admitting to them that I've taken on just too many things to be effective, and asking to be relieved of the responsibility.

Never be afraid to back out gracefully if you find you have gotten carried away with favors for people. Backing out just may be the best thing you could have done for that committee, because now they will be able to replace you with someone who can devote more attention to their endeavor.

Important: In eliminating nonpriority items from your list, remember that rest and relaxation are not necessarily secondary. How long has it been since you've broken away from the routine for some fun time with family or friends? Have you been uptight lately? Your body may be telling you that it's time for a rest. Be honest with yourself as you cross out the unessentials.

4. Put the remaining items in the order of importance.

Are there tasks which just can't wait any longer? Place the number "1" beside each of these items. Place a "2" beside those which need to be done very soon, a "3" beside those which need to be done as soon as possible, and so on. This procedure will prevent you from spending time today on low-priority items while very important ones stand waiting.

5. Delegate tasks if possible.

This does not mean to "dump" your responsibilities on another person simply because you don't wish to do them. To delegate is simply to admit that there may be someone either better qualified, or with more time for the task, than you.

If you have a secretary, for example, it would be a foolish waste of time for you to struggle at typing a business letter or report. She is trained for that sort of thing, and it's just good business to delegate a typing project to her. Likewise, your teen-age son may be handy at household repairs. If you're having a rough time getting around to installing the utility shelves, challenge your son with the task. Let him in on how you are trying to make the best use of your time—it will be a good learning experience for him, too.

6. Determine which items can be done as husband-and-wife or family projects.

Are you changing the oil in the Chevy this weekend? Maybe now's the time to teach Mike and Jim how to do it themselves. Or if you're finally going to refinish the antique cabinet, why not make a date with your wife to work at it together?

Household projects *can* be fun. I know a father who has perfected the art of holding family workdays. As each family member rakes leaves, washes windows, or weeds flower beds, he goes from one to another and works alongside each for a half hour or so. He uses this time to talk with each child about school, sports, boyfriends and girl friends— anything that comes up. Then, before he moves on to help the next person, he says, "You know, I really love you, and I'm glad you're *my* son (or daughter). Thanks for being such a big help today." At the end of the day—projects completed—the family votes on a special treat: root beer floats, miniature golf, swimming, or some similar celebration of a day's work well done.

That's one dad who is multiplying his time three ways. He's getting the chores done, teaching his children responsibility, and most important, growing closer to his family through communication and teamwork.

7. Schedule the items on a monthly and/or weekly calendar.

Scheduling is a good investment of time. Fifteen or twenty minutes of advance planning can be worth hours later on, for a good schedule will help you see at a glance:
   —what job you must do tomorrow, this weekend, or next week
   —when you should begin
   —when you need to be finished
   —whether your daily life is one of balance or chaos.

The monthly calendar on page 46 will help you see thirty days in advance the basic chunks of time that will be needed. You'll find it helpful to first list the things to be done at the top of the page under "PERSONAL," "FAMILY," "JOB," and "MISC." headings. Then, using pencil to allow for changes, schedule your month according to the numerical priorities you've already assigned each item.

When you have taken a look at what the next month holds, you'll want to get more specific. "*When* on the 22nd and 23rd will I make the time to write my speech? And what if some smaller emergencies come up, as they usually do?" To answer these questions, draw yourself a weekly calendar like the one on page 48.

You'll notice that the days are simply divided into "Morning," "Afternoon," and "Evening" rather than into half-hour and fifteen-minute segments. This brings up an important

SAMPLE MONTHLY SCHEDULE CALENDAR

FAMILY   PERSONAL   JOB-RELATED   MISC.

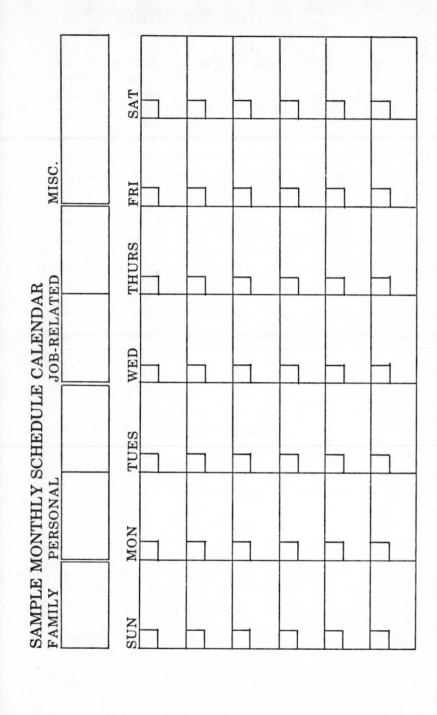

SUN	MON	TUES	WED	THURS	FRI	SAT

word of caution: Remember that a schedule is designed to serve *you;* you are not to serve the schedule. A schedule can either bind or free you. I used the fifteen-minute segment kind for several months, and for my tastes, it kept me glued to too rigid a routine. I found I was either running myself into the ground sticking to it, or feeling frustrated and guilty when I got behind. Some people work best under such a schedule, but I don't. Use your judgment as to which type best meets your needs.

On the weekly calendar you can get as specific as you like with your days. First, schedule in those things which are everyday experiences for you: grooming, dining, family activities, exercise time, office time, etc. Then, using your monthly calendar as a reference, determine which times of the day will be best to work at your special tasks.

I keep the monthly and weekly calendar right in front of me on my desk. Being organized, I've found, is one of the most relaxing feelings a busy man can have.

8. Stop procrastinating.

"The best way to get something done is to begin."

That little gem of wisdom has done wonders for me. I've been overheard repeating it to myself on more than one occasion as I struggled to launch into a project.

Starting is always the hardest part of any task, so BEGIN NOW—before you can think of any distractions.

9. Follow through with your schedule.

Once you have made out your schedule, *stick to it!*

Review your schedule frequently. Each evening, study your schedule for the next day to focus your mind on what you will be doing. Review it again in the morning. This will help keep you from getting sidetracked.

Then, devise little rewards for yourself. "When I finish this report, *then* I'll go get a cup of coffee." "After two more

SAMPLE WEEKLY SCHEDULE CALENDAR

	SUN	MON	TUES	WED	THURS	FRI	SAT
MORNING							
AFTERNOON							
EVENING							

phone calls, I'll go for a short walk." Sometimes the only reward necessary is the sheer delight of crossing an item off your schedule as "Done!"

10. Learn to say "No."

Many rush jobs or tempting opportunities will come your way as you seek to make the best of your time. If things are going well and you need a new challenge, then fine—have at it. But always measure the new job or opportunity against your set of priorities first.

Someone once asked former President Dwight D. Eisenhower how he managed to function with so many demands on his time. Said Ike: "I learned to distinguish between 'urgent' and 'important.'"

Think about that for a moment. Are all the "urgent" things that pull at us really the *important* things?

I once worked for a company whose field reps had a habit of requesting a writing project just a few days before they needed it in final form. The result was a lot of scurrying, several late evenings, and a couple of all-nighters.

Now I don't mind bending a little like that *if* the "urgent" project is really an important one. I began doing some serious thinking, though, when on three consecutive rush jobs I spent umpteen extra hours getting the jobs done, only to have the reps change their minds later and decide not to go through with the projects after all.

From those experiences I learned that most things labeled "urgent" are simply the result of poor planning. Handle them with caution. I have since been known to fire a job back to the originator and say, "Why the hurry? Let's take the time to do it right."

Whatever comes up, weigh it against your priorities. Is it really important, or merely "urgent" or flattering? If your schedule can't handle it, be gracious but firm in saying "No."

Time is given to us as a tool to use in experiencing the fullness of life. Learn to use it wisely, but never allow schedules or clocks to mechanize your daily life-style. We use minutes and hours to work hard, but minutes and hours are also available to help us slow down—to look, and perhaps see for the first time; to listen, and hear what God and our loved ones are telling us; to smell, touch, and taste a world waiting to be discovered.

Dietrich Bonhoeffer, who spent a good deal of his time locked in a prison cell, could have been uptight about all the time he was losing. But he had a different perspective. "Time lost," Bonhoeffer wrote, "is when we have not lived a full human life—time unenriched by experience, creative endeavor, enjoyment, and suffering."

So what's your hurry?

5 Your Personal Fitness Profile

I never run when I can walk. I never walk when I can stand still. I never stand when I can sit down. I never sit when I can lie down. Whenever I feel the urge to exercise, I lie down until it goes away.
ROBERT
MAYNARD
HUTCHINS

TV's David Frost was hosting a poolside party recently when one perceptive guest surveyed the group of sunbathers and quipped, "Why is it that almost all the men these days look pregnant?"

Look around the next time you're at a beach or swimming pool and see if you don't agree. Some of us won't even have to wait that long. In the office, on a downtown street, or in our own mirrors, it's only too obvious that we have let the soft society grab us by the seat of the pants.

I'm not sure why, but somehow we've managed to overlook the seriousness of the bulge. For one thing, it is almost assumed that a man working hard to provide a living is going to put on a little weight, especially at a desk job. Fat is just part of the price he pays.

But another, stranger phenomenon has taken place in that our culture has been deluded into thinking that fat is jolly. Santa is jolly. Big Uncle Herman is never without healthy, rosy cheeks and a tall

51

tale. Aunt Lotta makes jokes about how she can't squeeze into the restrooms on airplanes. In commercials, movies, and folklore, the roly-poly people are always the happy people.

The pathetic truth is that America is practically setting off earthquakes with its overabundance in poundage, and that obesity leads far more people to sadness than to bliss. Almost every overweight person *wants* to lose that weight, but the temptations of modern foods—combined with a sedentary life-style—make reducing a formidable battle. It is often difficult to find clothes which fit well. And usually the mirror is more depressing than encouraging.

But the outward signs of overweight, even if slight, are only symptoms of potential danger on the *in*side of the individual. Research shows that obesity is a direct or indirect cause of numerous other bodily ailments, both promoting the disease while prohibiting the cure. For example, those "healthy, rosy" cheeks could be a sign of overexertion of the heart. And Dr. Kenneth Cooper, author of *The New Aerobics,* observes:

> Heart disease is a national disaster. Every year, nearly a million Americans die from heart and blood vessel disease—a death rate higher than that of any other country.
> ...600,000, which adds up to one death every 50 seconds, [die] from coronary disease alone.

This kind of thing is not happening exclusively to the super-fat, because they often are cautiously watching out for it. Heart disease, lung ailments, and heart attacks are becoming more and more common to those of us just five, ten, and fifteen pounds overweight, and even to those whose weight is in control.

Dr. Cooper's statistics show that health—or the lack of it—needs to be a prime concern of every man living today. The body is a miraculous machine, so closely integrated with all that we are and do. Its health lends vitality to our alertness, relationships, and spiritual awareness as well as to our work and pleasures. Likewise, its softness causes a drowsy, dull, and often disoriented response to life.

The late John F. Kennedy put his finger right on the problem when he said, "We are underexercised as a nation. We look instead of play. We ride instead of walk. Our existence deprives us of the minimum of physical activity essential for healthy living."

I firmly believe that our society, so advanced in its medicine and technology, has advanced to the point of actual physical degeneration.

Contributing to our general decline in personal health, the following factors are almost unique to our generation:

A performance-oriented work and success ethic. In which jobs have become more and more deskbound while they have increased in pace and intensity. To achieve "success" one spends longer, harder hours without the physical labor which, in previous generations, served as a natural relaxant in the course of the day. The stresses of desk duties, combined with the resulting lack of exercise, foster increasing tension, fatigue, and obesity.

Closely related to this is *diet.* Our modern entrepreneurism has brought us coffee and a sweet roll for breakfast, a Big Mac and large fries for lunch, and mounds of pasta, potato chips, and Sara Lee German Chocolate Cake for dinner. At work we need only walk down the hall for a candy bar or ice cream sandwich, and of course we'll need soda pop or more coffee. On Wednesdays and Fridays we have business luncheons and dinners. During "off" evenings, well, a bag of potato chips would sure be nice for watching TV ... and a sandwich ... and a handful of those chocolate chip cookies ... and then to wash it all down....

Multiplied entertainment. The average American spends more time in front of a TV set than in any other activity besides work or sleep. Take an evening stroll through your neighborhood or apartment complex and notice how many living room walls reflect the pale light of the television set. And what's for entertainment outside the house? A professional football or baseball game, a movie, a play; dinner or a snack out—all sedentary occupations. For those who do desire some active recreation, it's difficult to get a group together, especially during *Starsky and Hutch* or *The Rockford Files*.

Air and noise pollution. The air in many of our nation's cities is so poisoned by the exhaust from autos and industry that it is often depressing just to step outside. Eyes burn from the irritants, breathing becomes heavy, and fatigue and headaches set in. In some cities, outdoor exercise is discouraged by smog alerts which caution people—especially children and heart patients—to remain inside an air-conditioned building.

And in spite of the warnings of the U. S. Surgeon General, smoking has continued on the increase. Dr. Thomas Mulvaney, of the Harvard Medical School, estimates that American smokers send nearly forty tons of solid air pollution into the skies each day in the form of smoke particles.

The pollution of our air combines with the modern cacophony from all sources: jetliners, lawn mowers, screaming children, angry parents, trucks, passing cars, blaring radios and TVs. Doctors are noting an alarming upswing in the frequency of hypertension, the heart and arterial disease brought on in part by frequent noise and stress situations. Without an escape valve, such tension can kill.

All of the above factors seem to contribute to a *decrease in motivation* for personal physical fitness. It isn't that modern man doesn't desire to be in good shape—physical fitness books have been on the bestseller lists for the past ten years. The problem, I'm convinced, is our "instant" improvement complex: If it can't be done immediately, it takes too long. In spite of the ads which claim, "I took ten inches off my waist in just fourteen days," getting and staying in shape takes time and discipline. And in the course of time, our desire for fitness falls victim to more immediate pursuits.

The human body is such an intricate mechanism that it comes equipped with all kinds of danger signals to let us know when it is being misused and abused. Some of us will not bother to heed those signals until we are flat on our backs. For others, there is an endless supply of pills which treat only the symptoms—not the root problems. We have pills for headache, backache, tension or chest pains, and pills to give us energy or sleep. Depending on them is like giving your car STP Gas Treatment when what it really needs is a complete overhaul.

What are those danger signals? To help you evaluate your own level of physical fitness, we've put several together in the form of a Personal Fitness Profile. Read each statement carefully, along with the implications which follow. Then mark T for True or F for False in the blank to the left of each statement.

YOUR PERSONAL FITNESS PROFILE

T/F

___ 1. *My job involves lots of sitting.*
We've already seen what today's office scenario can do to both the endurance and the waistline. If you are deskbound, keeping the tension and inches away will take some extra effort.

___ 2. *I often feel tense and jittery inside.*
When daily circumstances, details, problems, and countless-things-left-to-do become too much for you, your chest will often tighten and you'll feel on edge. Such prolonged tension can shoot your blood pressure sky-high, fray your emotions, and damage your heart.

___ 3. *I sometimes find myself "winded" after short bursts of physical activity (i.e., climbing a flight of stairs, walking briskly, etc.).*
This is a common sign of poor conditioning, in which your lungs are unable to supply enough oxygen to your heart and brain to meet the stress. The result is an out-of-breath feeling, a pounding heart, and light-headedness.

55

___ 4. *According to the insurance company charts, I am five pounds or more overweight.*

According to doctors, every pound of fat in the human body contains a mile of blood vessels. Therefore, every extra pound of fat you carry around is one additional mile of work for your heart. Since insurance companies bank on people staying healthy, their standards for desirable weights are worth considering. The chart below is adapted from the Metropolitan Life Insurance Co., New York.

DESIRABLE WEIGHTS
FOR MEN AGED 25 AND OVER*
in pounds according to height and frame,
in indoor clothing, and shoes

HEIGHT		SMALL FRAME	MEDIUM FRAME	LARGE FRAME
Feet	*Inches*			
5	2	112-120	118-129	126-141
5	3	115-123	121-133	129-144
5	4	118-126	124-136	132-148
5	5	121-129	127-139	135-152
5	6	124-133	130-143	138-156
5	7	128-137	134-147	142-161
5	8	132-141	138-152	147-166
5	9	136-145	142-156	151-170
5	10	140-150	146-160	155-174
5	11	144-154	150-165	159-179
6	0	148-158	154-170	164-184
6	1	152-162	158-175	168-189
6	2	156-167	162-180	173-194
6	3	160-171	167-185	178-199
6	4	164-175	172-190	182-204

*Adapted from Metropolitan Life Insurance Co., New York. New weight standards for men and women. Statistical Bulletin 40.3, Nov-Dec., 1959.

___ 5. *When I stand erect and relaxed and then look straight down, I cannot see my toes.*
A sure sign that your beltline is far more advanced than it should be. You are literally "watching your weight."

___ 6. *Twice or more in the past month, I have been frustrated at how my work seems to pile up on me.*
Anxiety over the job situation is an ever-increasing deterrent to health and well-being. Your frustration is an indication that your work may be taking too high a priority at this point in your life.

___ 7. *My resting pulse rate is more than 80 beats per minute.*
If your resting pulse rate is more than 80 beats per minute, it is compatible with a number of possible disease states, including hyperthyroidism. It's best to have your doctor evaluate your condition as soon as possible. Dr. Laurence E. Morehouse, author of *Total Fitness* and Professor of Exercise Physiology and Director of the Human Performance Laboratory at UCLA, has found that the average pulse rate for men is 72-76 beats per minute. "Resting rates higher than 80 beats per minute," he states, "are suggestive of poor health and fitness, and increased risk of coronary heart disease and death in middle age. The mortality rate for men and women with pulse rates over 92 is four times greater than for those with pulse rates less than 67."

___ 8. *When I took my pulse, my heartbeat was irregular.*
Says Dr. Morehouse, "Sickness is indicated by a too rapid pulse, or one that's not beating rhythmically." Irregular heartbeat warrants an immediate evaluation by your physician.

___ 9. *In the past month, I have been bothered by three or more headaches.*
Unless caused by an organic disorder, headaches are almost always the result of tension. What's bugging you?

___10. *My doctor has warned me about my blood pressure.*
While pressures from the outside world frequently have a bearing, high blood pressure is in most cases caused by organic abnormalities. High blood pressure may be the forerunner of heart disease, heart attack, stroke, or kidney failure. Fortunately, you can control high blood pressure with proper diet, exercise, medication, and outlook. Follow your doctor's recommendations religiously.

___11. *I haven't been to the doctor for a physical exam in the past two years.*
You're one year past due.

___12. *I engage in vigorous physical exercise fewer than two times each week.*
Not only does regular exercise help you to feel and look better, but recent studies by Drs. Cooper, Morehouse, and many others show that exercise increases strength and endurance while decreasing the chances of heart, lung, and stomach ailments. Most doctors agree also that the "weekend athlete" is only asking for trouble; most recommend a minimum of three times a week.

___13. *I am a smoker.*
Reports linking smoking to lung and throat cancer are well known by now, but recent studies also show that smoking just *half a pack* of cigarettes daily increases your risk of dying from heart attack by 60 percent; *one pack* a day increases your risk 110 percent. Yes, smoking *is* one of the hardest habits to quit.* But you'll love yourself for doing it. So will millions of nonsmokers.

*If you're serious about quitting, send for these excellent booklets: 1. *Me Quit Smoking? Why?* and *Me Quit Smoking? How?* Available from your local American Lung Association office; 2. *How to Quit Smoking By Really Trying—A Five-Day Plan.* Five-Day Plan, 6840 Eastern Avenue, N.W., Washington, DC 20012.

The American Lung Association reports that there is four times as much carbon monoxide in the side-stream smoke (from the burning end of a cigarette) as in the main-stream smoke inhaled by the smoker himself.

___14. *My diet frequently consists of breads, sweet treats (including drinks), potatoes, and pasta.*

If you'll observe the average housewife at the checkout line of the supermarket, you'll see first-hand evidence of how America has become sugar- and carbohydrate-oriented. Carbohydrates are generally the least expensive of foods—and also the least nutritious. Dr. Robert C. Atkins, author of the famous *Diet Revolution,* cites that "... a large number of doctors and medical researchers have observed that the overweight person, the diabetic, the hypoglycemic (that's a person suffering from a low level of blood sugar), the heart-attack prone, all have one thing in common: Something is very wrong with the way their bodies handle sugar and other carbohydrates."

Researchers are noticing more and more how large doses of sugars and carbohydrates actually *decrease* one's energy level, even to the point of drowsiness. And Dr. Laurence Morehouse adds, "Much of the cholesterol deposited in the blood vessels of inactive people is thought to be the result of an overabundance of sugar in the diet, rather than fat, as most people believe."

___15. *I usually eat six or more eggs each week.*

Eggs are one of the best forms of pure protein money can buy, but they also have the highest level of cholesterol, second only to liver and brains. Cholesterol is a waxlike substance which can build up in blood vessels and in the heart, blocking the crucial flow of blood and oxygen to the rest of your system. It is a prime cause of heart attacks. The Inter-Society Commission for Heart Disease Resources recommends that the average daily intake of cholesterol be reduced to less than 300 milligrams per day. One egg alone contains 252 milligrams.

___16. *I usually have four or more cups of coffee in a day.*

Anything over 250 milligrams of caffeine a day is considered a large amount, and each cup of coffee you drink contains close to 100 mg. There is evidence (though controversial at this point) that two or more cups a day increases the risk of heart attack, and other reports have produced evidence that coffee increases blood pressure. One definite correlation is that of caffeine and central nervous system disorders. The *Journal of the American Medical Association* reported that in one case, a nurse who drank ten to twelve cups of coffee each day had a three-week bout with headaches and irregular heartbeat. Her symptoms disappeared within thirty-six hours after she stopped drinking coffee.

___17. *My thighs feel soft and flabby.*

Dr. Paul Dudley White, the cardiologist who treated President Eisenhower, once said: "Before I consider heart surgery, I always feel the patient's thigh. If the thigh is firm, I know the surgeon is going to find a strong heart to work on when he gets inside. But if the thigh is flabby, the heart's going to be the same—and he's going to have problems."

___18. *I often have trouble sleeping peacefully.*

Everyone will have trouble occasionally, but chronic insomniacs are often the product of tense, overworked days. You are not alone—it is estimated that in the United States, 15 million sleeping pills are swallowed each night. *Don't* take pills regularly—most of them can produce serious, little-publicized side effects. In the next chapter we'll discuss some better ways of getting to sleep and staying there.

___19. *I often find myself getting sleepy and fatigued in the middle of the day.*

Another telltale sign that the diet, sleep, and endurance level aren't quite what they need to be.

___20. *I am usually so exhausted when I get home in the evening that all I want to do is go to bed or sit down in front of the TV set.*

We'll be showing you a good way to shake off that run-down feeling and enjoy the evening ahead of you.

___21. *I have noticed darkening circles under my eyes.*

Several factors contribute to the raccoon effect, among them insufficient sleep, eyestrain, prolonged illness, or a lack of sunshine, fresh air, and exercise.

___22. *My chest size is less than six inches larger than my waist.*

By no means would I become legalistic with the inches and centimeters, but if your tummy size *is* within six inches of your chest size it's a good indication of troubles in the rotunda. Body proportions are a relative thing, and you may be perfectly content with a beer-keg physique instead of a V-shape, but the above standard will help you see whether your stomach is getting too big for the rest of your body to support healthily.

___23. *In the past two years, I have gained two or more inches in my waist size.*

For all of us in the twenty-five-and-over crowd, those extra inches seem to climb onto us more subtly each day. If you've gained two inches in as many years, chances are good that you'll keep right on at the same rate unless you begin now to alter your life-style a little.

___24. *I just don't have the time to concern myself with physical fitness.*

You really don't *have* the time to shower, brush your teeth, and use the toilet in the morning, either. But what do you do? You *make* the time, because these little routines are a necessary part of being comfortable and presentable. Good physical exercise and common sense are no less necessary. A few hours spent each week can be considered an *investment* in a better quality of life. You'll find that all those tasks and causes you're running around trying to accomplish will get done so much easier when you're fit for the job. So if you don't have the time, *make* the time. If you don't, you may someday have more time than you know what to do with—in a convalescent bed.

When you have completed your Personal Fitness Profile, go back and add up the number of times you marked T. Now come the cold, hard facts: If your total is 10 or more, chances are you could stand to place a little higher priority on your personal physical fitness.

6 Your Personal Fitness Program

Perhaps you are one of the thousands with a string of twenty broken New Year's resolutions about getting more exercise. You've recognized the need for physical rejuvenation and launched into an intense program of jogging, weight lifting, or other insanity—only to peter out two or three weeks later.

The key to maintaining a good fitness program is to engage in a *fun* program. If you hate running in place, go bicycling instead. If you have trouble going it alone, find one or two faithful workout partners. There is tremendous encouragement and enjoyment in exercising as a group. The important thing is to find a form of recreation which will develop and relax you at the same time.

Sometimes the best way to stay disciplined is through a long-term commitment. A membership at the YMCA will serve as a year-round encouragement to regular exercise. A while back, when Kathy and I were both having trouble staying on a fitness program, we took out a membership at a local health club. It's one of the best investments we could have made toward progressive health, strength, and relaxation.

Then, be creative in making exercise a *family* activity. It's great fun for the kids, and something about these times brings the family closer together in love and sharing.

What's
Needed?

Leave the sub-four-minute mile and the 450-pound clean-and-jerk to the Olympic medalists—your goal is a healthy body, not a super-human one. Basically, a sound program includes some moderate muscle-strengthening exercises combined with a routine to increase cardio-vascular strength and endurance. The underlying principle which determines your progress is the principle of *progressive overload*.

"Progressive" is to keep you from overexerting yourself. Overexertion makes exercise a pain, and nobody enjoys pain. The zealous beginner who tries to run four miles a day his first week out will most likely stay in bed the second week. Go slow at first, and then gradually increase your pace or distance only as you become physically accustomed to your previous pace or distance.

"Overload" is simply doing a little more than you're accustomed to doing. For example, if you rarely walk more than one block at a stretch, a good beginning overload would be *two* blocks. When two blocks become too easy, increase to three.

Then, as your heart, lungs, and leg muscles adapt easily to that distance, you might begin walking those three blocks five or ten seconds faster each week. When that pace becomes too simple, start jogging slowly. Then, run. This is *progressive overload*.

What About
Existing Programs?

Let's look at three of the most popular ones.

The Royal Canadian Air Force 5BX. Selling well in bookstores for close to fifteen years now, the Royal Canadian Air Force exercise program consists of five basic exercises. These cover the major muscle groups of the body, plus a suggested schedule of jogging or running-in-place for the heart-lung system. A friend and I used this program to condition ourselves for a climb up Mt. Whitney, and we were pleasantly surprised at how well it worked.

As we progressed through the program, we experienced a real sense of accomplishment and renewed motivation in checking off each level of the charts. We found that it helped to keep our specific goal in mind—reaching the top of that mountain without first dropping dead of exhaustion. Each daily exercise routine lasted only eleven minutes (twenty if you include the necessary post-workout shower). The only drawback we found was that the running-in-place required by chart number four was too difficult (have you ever *tried* raising your knees waist-high for 300 steps?) and no fun at all. After we conquered Mt. Whitney, we both pooped out on the Air Force program.

The New Aerobics. Dr. Kenneth Cooper's studies on the effects of exercise on heart disease and related ailments deserve commendation. His program of aerobics has by now replaced the Canadian Air Force Plan as the credo for many in the armed forces and schools, and for individuals. Aerobics takes our *active* forms of recreation such as jogging, walking, bicycling, swimming, tennis, etc., and determines how much of each needs to be done in how much time to effectively increase cardio-vascular health.

I was first exposed to aerobics in a college fitness class. My routine consisted of a two-mile run three times every week, to be run in a time under fourteen minutes. I enjoyed it, felt better, and scored noticeable improvement on a fitness test given at the end of the course. My only complaint with aerobics is that it places little emphasis upon muscular development. My legs were in great shape, but I felt the need for some supplementary exercises to firm and tone the stomach, chest, and arms.

Total Fitness. Dr. Morehouse's research at UCLA comes together in an interesting and informative bestseller. *Total Fitness* challenges the concept that effective exercise means hours of slavish sweat and drudgery, and Morehouse supports his views with convincing clinical evidence. He recommends an exercise program that is perhaps the most moderate I have ever seen, and would thus be ideal for the man middle-aged or older.

Any of the above fitness programs would be good starters for you. Before launching into anything, however, *schedule that physical exam with your doctor.* Tell him of your desire to begin regular, moderately progressing exercise and ask him if your exam shows anything which might restrict you.

Then begin your program. Your routine should consist of 1) at least two basic exercises for your chest, arm, and stomach muscles, and 2) a free-style exercise period for your leg muscles, heart, and lungs.

Both the basic and free-style exercises should be done three to four times each week. Some men who follow this program prefer to select three alternate days of the week as their exercise days and do both in one day. Others may enjoy doing the basics on Monday, Wednesday, and Friday. and the free-style (with some light warmup exercises) on Tuesday, Thursday, and Saturday.

Basics for chest, arms, and stomach

For muscular strengthening and endurance, nothing at home beats the good ol' American pushup and situp.

On your first day, after some mild stretching to "loosen up," do as many of each as you can *without straining.* Then on subsequent days, as you begin to feel comfortable with that number, gradually add more. Keep adding repetitions as you progress, and you will begin to see the chest, arm, and stomach muscles firm up. Be patient with yourself—it will take time. But if you follow the principle of progressive overload (and are sensible with your diet) the fat will begin to burn off.

Free-style for leg muscles, heart, and lungs

When you've completed your pushups and situps for the day, go on to your free-style exercise for heart and lung conditioning. The amount of time you spend here will be determined by your previous conditioning and by the activity you select. Some possibilities:

> walking (briskly!)
> jogging
> running-in-place
> rope skipping
> swimming (laps; not diving or playing)
> handball, racquetball, etc.
> competitive basketball
> tennis (if vigorous)
> rowing
> bicycling (with a minimum of coasting)

Take it easy your first few days. Experiment a little to find out how much exercise stimulates without exhausting you. Your aims are to get yourself breathing deeply without gasping, and to increase your pulse rate for a good *five minutes or more* before winding back down. Apply the overload principle to your free-style exercise, too—but again, we stress, *gradually.*

A common mistake for the beginning athlete is to ignore the crucial *cooling down* period. After you've completed running a half-mile, for example, your tendency will be to stop all movement and lie down on the nearest patch of grass. Don't. After vigorous exercise, most of your blood is pooled in the legs, and it is necessary to keep that blood circulating upward. Coming to a complete, sudden stop may cause you to faint. After you've run, then walk awhile, until your breathing returns to normal. Cool down slowly, then treat yourself to a warm-to-cool shower.

That's the basic routine. You won't find it hard, as long as you take it gradually. And within two weeks, I guarantee you'll start to feel stronger, more energetic and alive.

What About My Diet?

Probably more books have been written on diets than any other subject. We've heard of the water diet, the grapefruit diet, the egg diet, the protein diet, the vegetable diet, the vitamin diet, and the roughage diet. Now weight-watching scientists have made a full circle: back to the balanced diet. Crash diets of any sort have proven a shock to the human system, depriving the body of essential nutrients. In moderation, portions of all the food groups are necessary for health—even for losing weight.

The foods that tend to give us men the most trouble are the *saturated fats* and *sugars and starches*. We might call them the "killer foods" because, when eaten in excess, they can do just that.

Saturated fats are any fats that remain solid at room temperature: all animal meats and fats; dairy products; hard margarine; solid shortening; hydrogenated peanut butter; chocolate; egg yolks; and foods made with these ingredients. The saturated fats contribute both flab and cholesterol to your system. Don't go overboard on them.

Sugars and starches are present in most of America's snack foods as well as in bread, jams, honey, flour, pasta, soft drinks, potatoes, beer, ice cream, and similar foods. It has been estimated that the average American consumes the equivalent of two pounds of sugar every week. Besides proving devastating to one's endurance and waistline, high levels of sugar have been linked with heart disease and intestinal cancer.

But What CAN I Eat?

Eat a little of everything, but A LITTLE. God created the balanced diet for man to enjoy, but he also encouraged the apostle Paul to write, "Do all things in moderation." That's the key to losing weight and staying healthy.

"Moderation" is often the main problem for weight-gainers, and if you're one of them you might find help in two very simple shape-up strategies which *do* work.

The first is a no-nonsense program recommended by doctors at Methodist Hospital in Indianapolis, Indiana. Titled "The Big Four,"* it is guaranteed to trim a pound of fat from your frame every week. The second shape-up strategy is what we'll call our "Maintenance" program. It contains guidelines to help you *keep* the new physique you attain through the Big Four.

"THE BIG FOUR"—
to get those unwanted pounds off

1. *No snacks.* Three balanced meals a day is healthy; anything eaten between meals will make you fat. (Zero-calorie snacks are allowed to help stave off hunger pangs.)
2. *No seconds.* Moderate first helpings at meals keep you alive; second helpings make you fat.
3. *No soft or high-calorie drinks* (especially beer). The average-size coke contains 150 calories. (Diet soft drinks are allowed.)
4. *Small desserts only.* One small helping of dessert will satisfy your sweet tooth; a regular-size helping will make you fat.

"Simple, yes," you may be saying. "But if you know me, it's also impossible."

It needn't be. Think of the Big Four as *temporary*—to be

*From *The Problem-Oriented Practice,* 1976, Methodist Hospital, Inc. Used by permission.

followed until you've lost the desired amount of weight. Then you'll put yourself on the "maintenance" strategy to keep those lost pounds from coming back. And in following the Big Four, you might find it helpful to adapt some of the maintenance guidelines suggested below (not including, of course, any which violate your Big Four regimen).

"MAINTENANCE" STRATEGY—
to keep those lost pounds from finding you again.

1. Try to plan your day so that your exercise will conclude about a half hour before mealtime. Exercise will flush the blood away from your stomach, leaving you less hungry for the upcoming meal, and you won't desire as much as you normally would.

2. Never go shopping on an empty stomach. Shopping while hungry will make the bakery or ice cream shop only more tempting, and if you're in a grocery store you'll be apt to pick up several "impulse" items you don't really need.

3. Eat your meals slowly. Savor every bite by chewing it thoroughly. Some successful dieters recommend putting your fork down between bites to force you to take your time while eating. You'll find that by slowing down, you'll be just as satisfied with less food.

4. Have a hot drink a half hour before a meal. Coffee, tea, or bouillon will take the edge off your hunger to help you eat less.

5. Wait at least twenty minutes for dessert—the Weight Watchers people say it takes at least that long for the stomach to signal the brain that it's full. You may decide you don't need dessert after all, and the interim time can be put to good use through family conversation, devotions, etc.

6. Nothing induces snacking like boredom, so keep your life interesting! Take up a hobby that will keep you from wandering into the kitchen every hour. Find some-

thing to do with your hands (besides eating) while watching television.

7. Before you snack, ask yourself, "Now why am I eating this?" What's causing it? If you've had a balanced meal within the last five hours, it isn't hunger after all. Is it boredom? Frustration? Tension? Take a quick about-face from the kitchen or vending machine, and go to work on the *real* reason for your snacking.

8. If you *must* snack, try to keep low-calorie, high-food-value items such as celery, carrot sticks, or cauliflower buds around. They can be just as satisfying as potato chips or sweet rolls, and the psychological lift of eating "healthy food" will make that satisfaction even greater.

9. Ask your wife to help you cut back on some of the more common sources of fat and cholesterol. Use margarine (some are cholesterol-free) instead of butter. You might want to cut back to three or four eggs a week. Have her buy only lean meats. Limit milk to one or two glasses a day, or train yourself to like the 2 percent or nonfat milk. Ask her to substitute fresh fruit for those high calorie desserts.

10. If you slip, don't give up. One orgy in chocolate cake or banana splits doesn't mean you're a hopeless cheat. Just put yourself back on the maintenance program immediately, and ask yourself, "What will I do to successfully resist the temptation next time?" Don't feel bad about treating yourself occasionally; it's when those treats become a *regular practice* that you know things are getting out of control again.

SLEEP
How Much and
How to Get There

Recently, some discoveries have been made about sleep that can save you and me from a lot of anxiety.

Ever since I can remember, I have had trouble sleeping well. I tend to take my problems and gripes to bed with me and lie there rehearsing what I will say if So-and-So ever does such-and-such to me again. Two or three hours after hitting the sack, I'll still be wide awake. *Oh, I hope I can get this job done tomorrow.* A trip to the refrigerator, then back to bed. *What am I going to do about this bill?* A trip to the TV set, just in time for the Star Spangled Banner and Moments of Meditation. Then I begin worrying about how little sleep I'm getting.

Kathy is just the opposite. She'll come to bed and announce, "I'm not sleepy," and then be sawing logs in three minutes. I lie there grinding my teeth at how hard *I* worked today and how hard I'm *going* to work tomorrow, and don't-I-deserve-to-go-to-sleep-as-easily-as-she-does? Which keeps me awake for several hours fighting off feelings of martyrdom.

It's a keyed-up world we're working in, and often it is difficult to turn off the flow of our minds in order to attain a good night's sleep. But doctors who study sleep have learned something important which has helped me quite a bit: We don't necessarily *need* eight hours' sleep every night. Every person is different. We should do our best to get a regular amount every night, but if we don't, we shouldn't worry about it.

This interested me, so I began reading more on the subject to see how other people conquered sleeplessness. There were as many remedies as there are for hiccups:

> read something soothing
> drink warm milk
> write your biography (see if *that* doesn't put
> you to sleep...)
> count sheep
> count dollar bills
> count backward from one hundred
> think of nothing

play soft music
sleep with your head at the foot of the bed, etc.

In the process of experimentation, I discovered some principles that began working for me. It is my contention that if they can cure *my* sleeplessness, they can cure anybody's.

Getting There
Involves . . .

First, *the knowledge of a day's work well done.* If I have done my very best at the tasks assigned me, if I have shown loving kindness with my family, if I have lived as a total, balanced man today, then I am at peace with myself.

Second, *putting worries in their place.* Countless annoyances will nudge at my consciousness, but I am no longer a worrier. Jesus Christ said, "Come unto me, you who are weary and heavy laden, and I will give you rest." He's speaking to *me,* today. So I tell him, "OK, Lord, I'm taking you at your word. *You* take care of my worries for me. I'm not going to think about them."

Third, *stopping my work and study in the middle of the evening, if not sooner.* Working at something stimulating beyond eight o'clock is a sure way to keep my mind going when I'm trying to turn it off. In mid-evening, I'll turn to something relaxing: a pleasant chat with my wife, a long walk, a novel to read.

Fourth, *a hot shower.* While in the morning I work the water temperature from warm to cold, tonight I will do just the opposite. The heat and steam will relax and soothe the tension in my back and neck, and help induce a mild feeling of sleepiness.

Fifth, *a little relaxation routine when I hit the sack.* After Kathy and I have said our good-nights, I put myself through the *Tenlax* method, described by Dr. Mangalore N. Pai in *Sleeping Without Pills:*

1. Lie on your back and close your eyes.
2. Deliberately tense your muscles.
3. Stretch both legs fully with toes strained to stiffness and pointing away from you.
4. Deliberately tense muscles of both legs as tightly as you can without bending knees; hold this position as long as possible.
5. Press back of knees down into mattress.
6. Let muscles slacken suddenly and go limp. Tense and relax muscles of legs six times.
7. With your arms lying by your sides, make their muscles tense. Clench hands as tightly as you can without bending elbows.
8. Suddenly relax and unclench your fists. Repeat this process six times.
9. If by now you do not feel sleepy, close eyes and roll eyeballs downward and inward as if trying to look at the tip of your nose.
10. With your eyes still closed, roll them upwards. Repeat these movements a few times, and sleep will overpower you.

Within minutes, I am usually asleep. But if not, I won't worry about it. Not any longer.

There you have it.

Regular exercise, a moderate diet, and relaxed sleep—you've heard of them all before, but I hope we've given you enough motivation and ideas to help you make them a part of your daily life.

We men haven't exactly been beautifying America with our bodies, but we can sure begin to change that.

Why not start now?

7 Man and the Fear of Failure

*There can be no
real freedom
without the
freedom to fail.*
ERIC HOFFER

For several months now, I have been ask-ing men from all walks of life to confide in me just one secret. "I'm curious," I would begin, "and you don't have to answer if you don't want to. What is your foremost secret fear?"

So far, not one has declined answering. And the decided majority have replied, "The fear of being a failure."

Since we men have been so conditioned to pursue success, it follows naturally that failure is to be regarded as the enemy. "There is no loneliness," writes Eric Hoffer, "greater than the loneliness of a failure. The failure is a stranger in his own house."

And failure can't get more personal. Sometimes it seems to almost laugh, deri-sively, at the one hope or dream which we have dared to make vulnerable for suc-cess' sake. And inevitably, failure seems to pull others, especially our loved ones, down with us.

But for all the energy we expend avoid-

75

ing failure, it's odd that we haven't yet arrived at an agreement on what failure *is*. I asked each of the men who had told me they feared being a failure to then give me their definition of the word. The result was a listing so varied it could fill two pages of my dictionary. Among the answers:

"Not providing for my wife and kids."

"Either losing my job, or not moving ahead to a better position and salary."

"Well, you can be a failure in many ways—in your business, in your marriage, in sex. They're all important."

"I'm a failure if I set out to do something and it doesn't happen."

"Failure to me is losing. I think it was Vince Lombardi who said, 'Winning isn't everything—it's the *only* thing.' I believe that. I don't want to be a loser."

"Not reaching my goals in life."

"Not getting married."

"I'm a failure if I'm given an opportunity and don't go after it right then and there."

"Seeing everything you've worked for collapse right in front of you."

In listening to each gentleman form his answer, I noticed that most became quite uncomfortable. This is normal; accepting failure is never easy, and thinking about it is often considered a bad omen. Louis Kronenberger aptly summarized the modern dread of failure when he wrote, "We are neurotically haunted today by the imminence, and by the ignominy, of failure. We know at how frightening a cost one *succeeds;* to fail is something too awful to think about."

Which is, I am convinced, exactly why we *should* think about it.

We are fleeing from an ill-defined specter which takes different forms for different people. Its form is usually the direct opposite of the individual's concept of success: If success means money, failure is then the lack of money; if the goal is position, then failure is the lack of position. Our definition of success determines our definition of failure, and the result is a confused insecurity that can haunt us.

So let's think about failure for a few moments. By confronting it, we can learn to respect what it is, to discount what it is not, and then learn to turn failure into an asset.

Four Causes of Failure

Remember the "tower of success" we constructed earlier? Each building block in that tower represents a facet of our life—an activity, possession, goal, etc., with which we surround ourselves.

You'll recall that first comes the important foundation, the *Fulfillment Needs* which give man a solid basis of personhood:

MENTAL	PHYSICAL	SPIRITUAL	SOCIAL (especially family)

Then come the *Survival Needs*—those aspects of life necessary for health, maintenance, and continuance:

	CAR	MONEY	POSSESSIONS	
FOOD	CLOTHING	HOUSE	JOB	

Then the *Wants and Desires*—those items and goals which are nice-but-not-necessary:

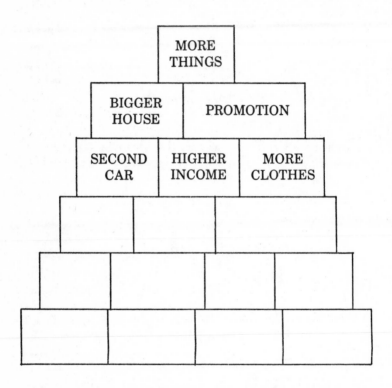

Such a tower is the portrait of the successful man—one who, like Christ himself, has his priorities in order and is living a balanced, fulfilled life.

Failure comes when we allow that tower to get off balance. It usually happens when, in setting our sights on a successful future, our aim becomes impaired by one of four common maladies:

Blindfold vision. The day in, day out existence of the man who has not set any worthy goals for himself. Gary Groper has been suffering from blindfold vision for years.

From the day he graduated, he knew he wanted to be a success—at what, he wasn't sure, but something would probably pop up.

So Gary began building his tower of success, one block at a time. At first, all that mattered was landing a good job, and when he found that, his next goal was a 280-Z. Had to have that car.

So for two years he worked extra hours, hard hours, so he could save enough for a down payment. And finally the "Z" was his (his and the bank's). Sure felt good to drive it.

But during the next couple of years a strange thing happened. The novelty of driving a 280-Z wore off. That which he had focused his whole life on was accomplished. Gary sensed the need for a new challenge.

A woman. How about making up for the social life missed because of all the hard work in recent years? So Gary Groper put a new wax job on the "Z" and began asking women to dinner, to shows, for 90 mph rides in the country.

It took him a while to realize he was spending so much money on his social life that he had to juggle all his credit payments. His new lack of funds started him daydreaming for a better job, for an inheritance from a long-lost uncle, *anything* better than what he had.

And for some reason, none of the women he dated seemed interested in anything permanent. The solution? Obviously, make more money.

79

THE TOTAL MAN

So Gary Groper committed himself to rising to the top. He worked his overtime where he was sure the boss would see him. He took courses at the university. He proposed new ideas for the boss's attention.

And Gary found himself rising from one tax bracket to the next. He even had his own secretary and country club card. But still, he was missing out on so many things: hobbies, a nice house, recreation, marriage, sports, more money.

Eventually, he would cover them all. One at a time. Finding temporary satisfaction, feeling permanent frustration ... Gary Groper spent life running blindly from one lucrative thing to another, seeking that euphoric feeling of "success."

His tower of success was a disaster. Because Gary had allowed his *Wants and Desires* to take top priority, he had not built a solid foundation for himself. The wants and desires actually *were* his foundation—a very inadequate one.

Acute near-sightedness. Building all of life upon one nonfoundational building block.

Aristotle Onassis, rest his soul, was a self-made victim of acute near-sightedness. It is estimated that this shipping tycoon was once worth one billion dollars. Onassis owned homes, villas, and apartments in half a dozen cities, a luxurious Ionian island, a priceless art collection, and the world's most lavish yacht—the 325-foot *Christina,* complete with luxurious bathrooms outfitted in Sienna marble and gold-plated faucets.

If he had been an American, we probably would have called him "the Great American Success Story." Aristotle Onassis had climbed from being an impoverished young man with only $60 in his pocket to one of the world's wealthiest. He was rarely without beautiful and famous women around him. A bachelor until age forty, Onassis's first marriage was to the seventeen-year-old daughter of another shipping tycoon. It wasn't long until he began a ten-year affair with opera singer Maria Callas. And by 1968, he was pursuing Jacqueline Kennedy.

While Onassis's life-style reflected his philosophy of life, his words echoed it: "All that really counts these days is money," he proclaimed. "It's the people with money who are the royalty now." In his fervor for money (and all it could buy), Aristotle Onassis built his entire life on one building block that wasn't really foundation material. He began feeling the load in 1973, when, as *Time* magazine reports it:

"(Onassis's) life changed dramatically ... when his son Alexander was killed in a plane crash. 'He aged overnight,' observed a close associate. 'He suddenly became an old man.' In business negotiations he was uncharacteristically absent-minded, irrational and petulant."

His son's death was like a snapping jolt to a man so protected from life's unpleasantries. Rumors began to circle the world that the tycoon's health was failing, that Onassis was deluged by a flash flood of guilt over his son.

Perhaps Onassis was realizing that he had been living life desperately out of balance. Whatever was on his heart, his

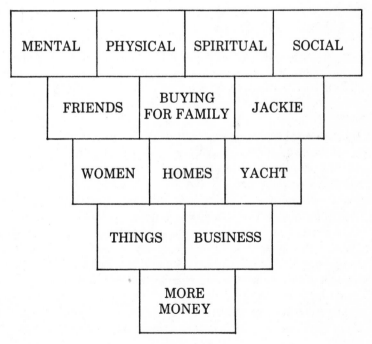

"foundation"—that one misplaced building block called "more money"—was crumbling.

As his health failed, his business acumen failed; concurrently, the Arab oil prices hit his shipping industry hard. *Fortune* magazine reported that Onassis's assets plunged from an estimated one billion to $200 million during his last year alive.

Death claimed him in March of 1975. Despite his last year's losses, Onassis was still a smashing success by society's standards—you can't really scoff at $60 parlayed into $200 million. But to those more interested in character than in counting, Ari's success is questionable. The man who had built a shipping dynasty had built his personal foundation of the wrong material, as illustrated on page 81.

Spotted vision. This common impairment sometimes occurs in those with the best of intentions. Perhaps we have seen the importance of *being* a well-balanced person, and have laid such a foundation for our "tower." At the base are our four basic building blocks:

1. Mental development and utilization toward wisdom
2. Physical development and fitness
3. Spiritual growth
4. Social relationships (especially intra-family)

This foundation represents our foremost goal in life: to be a total man, developing to our maximum capacity in *each* of these areas of life. On such a foundation we build our Survival Needs, and then our Wants and Desires. It looks like we're headed in the right direction. But soon we find ourselves loafing in one or two basic areas.

Let's take a common example: Suppose we get so enraptured with mental stimulations, spiritual things, and social activities that we shove physical fitness aside. "I know I should be exercising," the victim of spotted vision says, "but I just haven't had time." For two or three weeks, he doesn't really notice any adverse effect. But after a few months, the body begins to weaken. Endurance is noticeably decreased.

And the weakened body begins to affect the quality of his mental, spiritual, and social output.

In short, ignoring the physical foundation block of total manhood requires the other foundation blocks to bear more than their share of the load. The problem is only compounded if we concentrate on two facets, or three, while ignoring the others. Spotted vision, the pursuit of several worthwhile goals while ignoring others, is a chief cause of weakened, crumbling foundations in the tower of success.

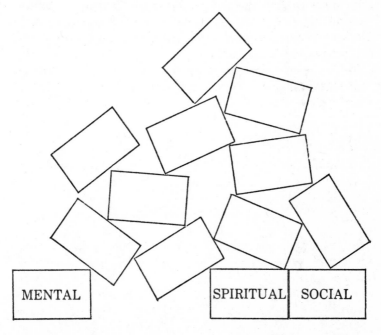

Tunnel vision. We see this impairment most in people dedicated to a cause, though tunnel vision is not necessarily exclusive to them. Tunnel visionaries live life in hot pursuit of *one* worthwhile, foundational goal at the near exclusion of the others.

Take Sam Savage, ace body builder and physical fitness nut. Sam has devoted almost every day since puberty to developing his biceps, triceps, lats, pecs, and traps to the maximum. He spends $20 more per week on foods than the average person, because his grains, milk, vegetables, and eggs must be organic. The vitamins—all natural—are taken in megadoses.

The extent of Sam Savage's extracurricular reading is *Strength and Health* and *Iron Man* magazines. His social life centers around the gym and the beach; in both places his best communication is with the weights he pumps around.

Someday, though probably not until he has won the Mr. Universe title, Sam Savage will discover that he is very lonely and unfulfilled. But because he has spent more effort on a balanced diet than on a balanced life, he'll have a hard time knowing what to do about it. In most cases like Sam's, the victim of tunnel vision can only go on in his chosen specialty, inventing even greater challenges.

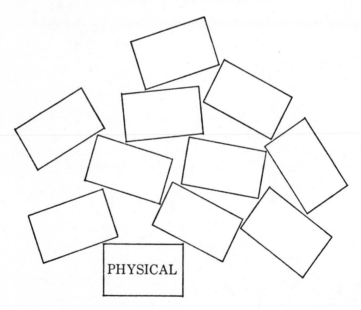

Among the victims of tunnel vision you'll also find the socialites who shine at gatherings but can't face being alone;

the ingrown bookworms who hide in the hardcovers to compensate for their lack of social graces, physical prowess, or spiritual awareness; and even some of the very spiritual people who have the highest calling in the world but have somehow missed God's call to a life of personal balance.

Like spotted vision, tunnel vision is often the disease of the well intentioned. Their concentration on one phase of foundational development places undue strain on the other three. Inevitably, the whole tower, the whole person, will suffer from the extra load.

Blindfold vision, acute near-sightedness, spotted vision, and tunnel vision all point up the deeper significance of failure. It goes beyond a surface setback such as a financial loss or an overlooked promotion.

To be a failure is to be less than a total man.

A failure is one who lives life out of balance, placing undue emphasis on one or two facets of life (or hopping from one to another) in that constant quest for fulfillment. Some of the richest men in the world are failures because they have failed to develop as *balanced persons.* Some of the world's greatest businessmen are failures because they have built their entire lives on inadequate foundations.

But we who embrace the Liberated Man's Definition of Success are fortunate. Our success or failure does not depend upon the fluctuations of the stock market, the boss's mood, or our access to a 280-Z. We are the sole determinants of our success or failure because God has given us the free will to choose whether we will build—and maintain—a foundation of total, balanced manhood.

You Can Fail
Without Being
a Failure

One very liberating truth is the fact that there is a great difference between *being a failure* and *experiencing failures.*

In spite of our best intentions, it's inevitable that we will sometimes let ourselves down. We may let our job keep us away from the family too long. Financial worries may detract from our trust in God. Our work for the company or the church might become so strenuous and time-consuming that our physical health suffers.

If you should ever find yourself slipping into the failure syndrome, congratulations—you have caught yourself. Many men do not. You have experienced failure, but you have not *become* a failure unless you ignore the lesson that your experience holds. A man will fail many times in living the complete life; he is only a failure, however, if he *continues* to live life out of balance.

Indeed, the true successes are those who have allowed failure to educate them. "We learn from failure," wrote Samuel Smiles in *Self-Help*, "much more than from success. We often discover what will do, by finding out what will not do; and probably he who never made a mistake never made a discovery."

Turn Failures
Into Victories

To utilize an old saying, if you have caught yourself in the act of failing, that's half the battle. You have admitted to yourself that your life, at that moment, lacks completeness. You want to put the foundation back in order.

To turn that failure into a victory, follow these six steps:

1. *Isolate the type of failure.* Which of the four "vision impairments" hindered my aim? And specifically, which building block received undue emphasis? Was it part of the Foundation? The Survival Needs? The Wants and Desires?

2. *Evaluate the consequences.* What other facets of life have suffered because of the misplaced priority? My relationship with God, my family? My health? My mental development?

3. *Ask: "What am I to learn from my failure?"* Thomas

Fuller wrote, "Wisdom rises upon the ruins of folly." Learning from failure usually takes the form of first a negative, then a positive declaration: "That I should not—and will not—spend so much time in front of the television set. That I should—and will—spend that time more creatively with my wife and children."

4. *Make restitution where necessary.* It is at this point that I often wish I were infallible. Most likely, my failure has affected someone else.

Because Kathy is so close to me, she is often the one who suffers from my lack of balance. In making things right, there is no substitute for total honesty: "Kathy, I've blown it. I've been so wrapped up in all my projects the last few weeks that our relationship has suffered. I'm sorry. Will you forgive me?"

It is often most difficult, though, to forgive myself. I'm angry for letting myself fail. It's hard on my ego, and if I've listened to society around me, my failure is a threat to my masculinity. A man doesn't fail, right?

Wrong! Here is where I must learn not to take my failures so seriously. I must learn to laugh at myself—to admit that I am still a clumsy adolescent at life, still and forevermore in the process of learning.

5. *Plan how you'll get moving again.* Make a list of ways to improve in the area you've slighted, *being careful not to slight the other areas in the process.* If I have been ignoring mental development and physical fitness, I will plan a balanced program for a fresh start. Perhaps two good books a month, and a vigorous set of tennis three times a week. This will still allow plenty of time for spiritual growth and family fulfillment.

6. *Move ahead ... and forget.* Put the plan into action, forgetting all the embarrassment, guilt and frustration over the failure. All is forgiven and forgotten; I have learned a great lesson. I am a stronger man now because I have not let the failure gain control of me. I have instead harnessed it to further ensure my success as a total man.

8 The Ultimate New Year's Resolution List

Good resolutions are useless attempts to interfere with scientific laws.
OSCAR WILDE

"I will live a more balanced life..."

Hmmm, not bad for a start. Now let's see...

"I will lose fifteen pounds this year...

"I will be more disciplined with my time..."

Discipline, yeah ... but didn't I write that one down last year?

"I will try to be more loving...

"I will spend more time with the children..."

Uh, oh, there's another one. More time with the kids. Was that last year, too? Or the year before?

"I will conquer my temper problem...

"I will try to be more relaxed..."

Now I *know* that one's a repeat. Relax? With *my* schedule? Well, we'll try it again...

New Year's resolutions. Have you ever tried to keep them?

Sure, we all have. Many times. We're gluttons for that annual exercise in futility. There's something about the turn of

89

the calendar that causes many of us to look inward for a few uneasy moments, to face up to our failings, and to pen a wishful phrase or two about what we *should* be. But *keeping* those resolutions, well...

Perhaps you're like the man who diligently made out his list on December 31, then diligently tossed it in the waste-basket on February 1. "I've already blown 'em all," he said. "In fact, I'd blown nine of them before the Rose Bowl came on."

Why are such self-improvement resolutions so difficult for us to keep? Why are they such serious business on December 31 and just an uncomfortable laughing matter a few days later?

The answer is simple, but in it lies a gold mine. If you'll grasp this answer and apply it to everything you read in this book—and to every challenge you encounter in life—you'll have found one of the most vital keys to a successful life and marriage.

Already, some of the concepts we've presented may have left you hesitant. "The balanced life sounds good," you might be thinking, "but I find it impossible to focus on the physical, mental, social, and spiritual dimensions of life all at once—especially when the world around me emphasizes a totally different set of values."

I agree. Living the balanced life, with all priorities in order, *can* be difficult. That's probably why so many have fled the challenge, to nestle themselves in mediocrity.

And living out those New Year's resolutions can be just as hard. If the wastebasket is any indication, all those charac ter qualities we commit ourselves to each January (and June, and November) are often just short-lived pipe dreams.

If that isn't discouraging enough, the Bible also gives a list of ideal personality traits that bears striking resem-blance to our own impossible dreams. We might call them "The Ultimate New Year's Resolution List." Written just under 2,000 years ago, the list gives us nine specific attri-butes that could, if they were attainable, bring the greatest possible fulfillment to ourselves, our families, our careers. But get a load of these:

    love
    joy
    peace
    patience
    kindness
    goodness
    faithfulness
    gentleness
    self-control

Sure—*sounds* great! Who wouldn't want to be a man with those character qualities in his life? But they're the same things we've been wishing and vowing every New Year's —there's no way we can do all that by ourselves!

If that is your conclusion, friend, you have just hit upon one of the greatest discoveries you'll ever make.

God doesn't expect you to do it all by yourself.

He doesn't want *anyone* to live in continual frustration, or to simply play-act when it comes to living the balanced life. That's the greatness of the whole divine story. He never asks us to do or be anything that he hasn't already provided the *means* for.

To illustrate: Picture for a moment a newborn son of your own. You're proud of this miracle of love between you and your wife. You want the very best for him—good clothes, food, education, shelter, and much more. You want your son to be able to survive the bumps of life—to learn and grow into a wise, strong man. Happy. Fulfilled.

So what do you do with him? Leave him all alone to fend for himself? Of course not. As his father, you'll guide him, provide for him, teach him, and set an example for him. He learns from watching you. Frightening, huh?

The point is: If you would do all this for your son, would our own Creator do any less for us? He holds a pretty high stake in our future. Because he wants the very best for us, nothing pleases him more than to see us grow in completeness and in character.

So, just as you would do for your own son, God has provided us with both the *means* and the *example*.

Jesus Christ, our perfect example of rugged maleness, was the only person ever to live without sin. He never "fell short." So, even though he was tempted just as we are, he is the only perfect example of love, joy, peace, patience, kindness, goodness, faithfulness, gentleness, and self-control.

And he is also our God-given *means* for attaining those same impossible qualities. The Bible calls that ultimate resolution list the "fruit of the Spirit." In other words, those fabulous character qualities are not attainable through any finite human effort, but are the natural by-product of a life which is focused on the infinite Jesus Christ.

We may as well forget trying to produce the "fruit of the Spirit" through our own striving. Not even positive thinking, possibility thinking, positive mental attitude, or positraction are the final answer. The fruit of the Spirit is far beyond the grasp of the one who thinks that simply gritting his teeth and repeating fifty times into the mirror "I *will* be joyful, I *will* be joyful, I *will* be joyful" will bring genuine joy into his life.

The apostle Paul, in an excellent portrayal of the frustration that man finds in trying to live these attributes on his own, wrote:

> I don't understand myself at all, for I really want to do what is right, but I can't.... When I want to do good, I don't; and when I try not to do wrong, I do it anyway (Romans 7:15, 19, TLB).

Sound familiar? Paul is writing about some very real-life situations here. We might compare them with those trying times we encounter every day, such as:

> How can I be loving to my wife when her hair's in rollers? Or when, during those certain times of the month, she gets difficult to live with?

NEW YEAR'S RESOLUTION LIST

How can I keep from getting so angry at little things?

Why do I get so impatient with the children?

Why do I keep getting uptight about our finances?

How do I fight the temptation to lust after another woman?

When such situations bombard us every hour of the day, there is no way that even the most alert, "good" human being can be consistently loving, joyful, peaceful, patient, kind, good, faithful, gentle, and self-disciplined. Paul couldn't, and he freely admitted it. He knew his limitations. Like all of us, he was just too weak ... too human. "There is something deep within me," he wrote, "... that is at war with my mind and wins the fight and makes me a slave to the sin that is still within me..."

But God is looking for strength of character. In his sight, weak character means a weak *person:* "Man looks at the outward appearance, but the Lord looks at the heart" (1 Samuel 16:7). So God provided Paul—and all the rest of us—with the answer to self-limitation and human weakness. "Who will free me from my slavery to this deadly lower nature? Thank God! It has been done by Jesus Christ our Lord. He has set me free."

Would you like to see victory over your self-limitations? You can!

Remember: God specializes in the impossible. He doesn't expect you to do it all by yourself—he wants to do it *in* you. *All the principles and guidelines in the Bible, in* The Total Man, *or anywhere else will only snow you under if you try to live them with only your human effort.* But if you trust God to work out these qualities in your life, he will remind, nudge, and instruct you as they become more and more a natural part of your thoughts.

Gradually, you'll be able to see a growing desire and discipline for living the balanced life. You'll realize a closer love relationship with your wife and children than you ever thought possible. You'll find yourself taking on an exciting new dynamic, because God is making you into his kind of man.

Many of the positive thinking and self-improvement books—after obligingly referring to God, or an "Infinite Intelligence," or a "Supreme Being"—will stop right there. "Trust God."

It sounds good. But then the reader begins thinking in practical terms. Like, "How? How does a human being 'trust God'? And what on earth does it mean to 'focus on Jesus Christ'?"

Valid questions. They deserve answers. And when today's self-improvement books simply say "Trust God" without telling *how,* it's like my giving you a beautiful, powerful new car but saying, "Oh, *by the way,* there's no key to it. You'll have to find a key or make one yourself—*then* you'll be able to use the car."

Fortunately, it isn't that difficult at all. Just a little further research on the part of those authors would have revealed that the key to "trusting God" lies in two simple, life-changing principles.

In the next chapter, we'll see how practical those principles are.

9
Break Free from Self-Limitation

*And you shall
know the truth,
and the truth
shall make
you free.*
JESUS CHRIST,
John 8:32

Why is it that we men tend to be cautious about the concept of trusting God?

One of the main reasons is that we've "framed" him. In striving to assert our independent masculinity we've trumped up some charges against God that simply aren't true.

Specifically, many men today have indicted God on two false accusations: 1) that he is only for women, sissies, and ignorant people who need an emotional crutch, and 2) that he is a negative force who wants to spoil everyone's fun and cause them to live in poverty.

Both observations are as shallow as they are stupid.

David, one of the greatest of earthly kings, and whom history shows was definitely no sissy or ignoramus, wrote: "Commit everything you do to the Lord. Trust him to help you do it and he will" (Psalm 37:5, TLB).

Solomon, perhaps earth's wisest and richest king, had no need of any "crutches." But he said:

95

If you want favor with both God and man, and a reputation for good judgment and common sense, then trust
the Lord completely; don't ever trust yourself. In everything you do, put God first, and he will direct you
and crown your efforts with success (Proverbs 3:4-6,
TLB).

In the course of my work, I have personally visited with
scores of dynamic businessmen, community leaders, professional athletes, and other men who were miles from effemi-
nate, ignorant, or emotionally weak—but who professed a
solid trust in God for their everyday lives. The sissy syndrome and the "I-don't-need-God" attitude just don't apply
to them. They've *seen* him produce the qualities in their own
lives that fifty years of New Year's resolutions had failed to
generate.

Observing David, Solomon, and men just like them has
taught me one important lesson: *The wise man is the one
who knows, and admits, his limitations.* There's nothing
unmasculine or ignorant about being honest with oneself.
We can't be God. And we simply cannot live the quality
of life without him that we can *with* him. That's why these
smart men, and millions of others, refuse to frame God on this
first false charge—they've discovered that *God only wants
the very best for them.* "And we know that all that happens
to us is working for our good," the Bible promises, "if we love
God ..." (Romans 8:28, TLB).

Regarding the second indictment: Is God *really* a negative
force? A giant Cosmic No-no? Let's go back to the father-son
illustration for a moment.

Suppose your children came to you and said, "Dad, we love
you so much for being our dad. It's easy to forget sometimes
how much you love us and sacrifice for us. And because we
love and trust you, we want to ask you to teach us how to be
good children."

After you picked yourself up off the floor, what would be
your response? Would you say, "Aha! Now I've got you! I'm
going to make your life so miserable! I'm going to keep you

locked in the closet, keep you from earning any money, dress you in drab clothes, and keep you from having any fun! You're going to regret your decision to trust me"?

Or would you say, "Children, I love you, too. And you've made me very proud today. In fact, you've made me so happy that I'm going to do everything I can to make life a rich, happy experience for you. I'll show you how to be wise, strong, successful people—filled with love for others"?

I hope your choice is obvious. But absurd as the first response sounds, it is what we have so often accused God of saying to those who trust him with their lives. We've framed God, accused him of being a negative, spiteful being when in reality he says to us, "I came that [you] might have life, and might have it *abundantly*" (John 10:10, italics mine).

Do you realize what *"abundantly"* means? It tells us that no matter how great we think life is, no matter how good we think we are, a life focused on Christ will be even *better*. *More* full. *More* meaningful.

Does that sound negative or spiteful to you?

I believe these "indictments" against God are simply smoke screens that man has fanned in order to avoid admitting human limitations. We'll cling to one weak argument after another to keep from facing the fact that we do have a spiritual dimension in our lives—a dimension which we've tried to fulfill in hundreds of synthetic ways.

But as French physicist/philosopher Blaise Pascal has observed, "There is a God-shaped vacuum in the heart of each man which cannot be filled by any created thing, but only by God the creator, made known through Jesus Christ."

A God-shaped vacuum. In other words, Pascal is saying that *every man, whether he admits it or not, has a deep-down need for intimacy with God.* When that need is unfulfilled, man is left frustrated in the relative shallowness of his purpose, his goals, his relationships. And though he'll try to put career, power, sex, money, things, macho, and good works into that God-shaped vacuum, *nothing short of God himself can fill the need.*

The God-shaped vacuum. That's the "favor with God" dimension that Christ exemplified, one of the four essential foundation blocks on our tower representing the complete life. God has designed you and me with a built-in dependency on him so that we'll place our trust in him. He simply wants us to say, "Father, we love you for loving us. And we want you to guide and teach us how to live a fulfilling, meaningful life." And if we trust him, he *will* teach us— through his Word, through other Christians, through supernatural prompting—how to live life with our priorities straight ... how to make wise decisions ... and how to let those impossible character qualities break through our human weaknesses.

Are you willing to let God fulfill the God-shaped vacuum—to make you into his kind of man?

Here are two simple but life-changing principles to show you how.

ONE
Make Sure
You Are
a Christian

Unfortunately, God has been framed on this one, too. Instead of simply trusting God, we've manufactured various ways of "being Christian." Some of us will say, "My parents were Christian, and this is a Christian nation, so therefore *I'm* a Christian."

Is a cat born in a bread pan a *biscuit?*

Others of us are convinced that being a Christian comes from doing good deeds, donating to charities, being emotional, praying grandiose litanies and prayers, attending church, serving on committees, teaching a Sunday school class.

Not necessarily so. You see, there is a world of difference between being "religious" and being a Christian.

The hypocritical Pharisees of Jesus' time were probably the most religious men on earth, yet they completely missed out on the truth. They thought that doing good deeds and following hundreds of stringent little rules was going to find them favor with God. Today, many men try the same exhausting approach.

But one of the things which made Jesus Christ such a dynamic, "liberated" man was his downright rejection of the ritualistic *got-to's* and *can't-do's* of religion. Men had been adhering to these petty rules for so many years that they had long been worshiping the *rules* instead of God. And since Jesus was literally God in human form, the leaders of his day couldn't recognize him—they were too busy with their rules.

So Christ outdated religion. His life, death, and resurrection provided a much more practical way for men to know God. Not religion, but a personal *relationship*.

Someone has aptly said that *religion* is man reaching and striving to find God; *Christianity* is God taking the loving initiative to find man.

In Jesus Christ, God took the initiative to fill the vacuum. Christ died on the cross as the last sacrifice that would ever have to be made for man's sin. God was saying, in effect, "I don't care how undeserving, selfish, or stubborn you are ... I love you! I want you to have the joy you've been searching for!" That verse we've all learned at one time or another takes on real significance here: "For God so loved the world, that He gave His only begotten Son, that whoever believes in Him should not perish, but have eternal life" (John 3:16).

That's what being a Christian means: *simply believing in Jesus Christ as the only way to satisfy our inborn spiritual dimension.* Good deeds, manmade religions, mere church attendance, and personal piety aren't adequate. "I am the way, the truth, and the life," he said. "No one comes to the Father, *but through Me*" (John 14:6).

Before learning this liberating truth, Pasadena marketing executive William Converse Jones tried every other conceivable approach. He tells it this way:

"I had finally achieved the goal of having my own advertising agency! Located in Beverly Hills, our firm handled

THE TOTAL MAN

public relations and advertising for leading subdividers and building material companies. Years of hard knocks (I was 38 at the time) and experience had spawned this agency and I was proud of it.

"It was satisfying work. But in the course of it, even *I* had noticed that I was becoming very cynical. As a salesman, I was good at manipulating people—a practice that was both stimulating and distasteful to me.

"Ironically, I was also very proud of my integrity in business dealings. But soon I learned the hard way that anyone will let down his standards in a tight enough situation.

"That same year, a big client refused to pay his bills and our ad agency developed serious fiscal trouble. The different businessmen our client owed money to formed a consortium of strength, and we demanded our payments together. But when the chance came, we as an agency abandoned our associates and took advantage of a handsome deal that was offered to us by the client's business manager.

"When I agreed to let the deal go through, something died within me. My desire to be in the advertising business died at that point, too. I had been a real 'power of positive thinking' person and had read all those books on envisioning your goal and then driving for it. I left the agency a disillusioned man.

"So when I saw that mere positive thinking didn't really work, I decided to take advantage of the double-indemnity clause on my insurance policy. My plan was to have a fatal accident on the freeway over the Thanksgiving weekend. But as the day approached, a little thought nagged at me: 'Suppose that after you die you have total understanding and discover that you missed the "answer"?'

"Realizing that I'd never taken the time to work out a personal philosophy, I took on the project in much the way that I used to take on a client's marketing account in the industry. I decided that if I couldn't find the answer to life in ninety days, then there wasn't one. I went out and got a good job and spent my evenings researching at libraries and bookstores or interviewing some successful man I admired just to see what made him tick. I became a student of the various popular religions and even read the Bible occasionally.

"In my search, I was ruthless and threw out anything that wasn't logical or useful to a businessman. It was a businessman's philosophy that I was trying to get, and if it was viable, then I thought I might even package it and share it with other businessmen.

"Before long, my ideas were ready to share with a lifetime friend named Hal Leford. He was a businessman in Los Angeles, too, and when I called, he promised to be a kind, gentle sounding board. I was really proud of the philosophy I had developed and it took me an hour and a half to get it all out.

"His response? 'Bill, you've got some good stuff there,' he said, 'but you've left out the main ingredient—Jesus Christ.'

" 'Weren't you listening?' I demanded. 'I've got the Sermon on the Mount, I've got the Golden Rule—why, I've got all the principles of Christianity in there.' Hal simply said, 'I'll grant you that, but you've left out Jesus.'

"I was really mad, but he promised not to mention it again if I would go to a Christian Businessmen's breakfast. I didn't argue—my only question was: Why didn't I hear about this before?

"I began going every Thursday and was astounded. Each week the speaker was a different man from a different business, and it was obvious that the faith they had was working for them. They all said that they knew Jesus Christ personally, and, as a result, they not only had proper business principles, but they were experiencing peace in the rat race of the business world.

"In June of 1965, Whitney Lyon, an investment banker and walking paraplegic, spoke. At the end of his testimony, there was so much joy in the room you could cut it with a knife. I went up to see him afterward and said, 'Mr. Lyon, I'll say it like I feel it. You have very little to be happy about, and yet you're a totally happy man. I have everything to be happy about, and I'm miserable. Why?'

"Mr. Lyon knew just how to handle me. 'Jones,' he said. 'I've heard about you. You're the resident skeptic and your guard is up. You also want to earn your place with God. Why, you make having your sins forgiven and finding peace with God so complicated that only Cal Tech professors could become Christians!'

"I couldn't argue because he was right. So he continued, 'Since you won't let anybody else lead you to Christ, how about if I explain how you can do it yourself? Tonight, after your family's gone to bed, get down on your knees and just tell God that you agree with him that you've fouled up your life—that's called repentance from sin. Then ask him to come into your life and take over. Tell him that you're giving him a lifetime management contract. Thank him for doing it, and get up and go to bed.'

"That night I followed his instructions to the letter. It took a couple of days before I noticed any changes in myself. But I gradually began to understand the Bible when I read it. And, most amazing, the lonesomeness that I'd always felt left me. My attitudes toward business began to change, too, and I became more people-oriented and began putting more weight on the people factors in my business decisions.

"... In the past ten years as a Christian businessman, I've experienced enough quiet miracles to fill a book. My relationship with God is not only viable but vital to my business and personal life.

"The problem is that most of us like to make things more difficult than they are. This includes the ways we try to earn acceptance and peace with God. All it really takes is that one eternal transaction—accepting his loving, all-wise control in exchange for our imperfect, limited self-control. Believe me, it's a management contract I'll never regret.'"*

The "lifetime management contract," as William Jones calls it, is simply the act of *receiving* Jesus Christ as per-

*This story, and those of Greg Brezinᴇ and John Bramlett, are adapted by permission from *Worldwide Challenge* magazine, Copyright © Campus Crusade for Christ International.

sonal Savior and Manager. Mere intellectual assent or emotional experiences won't do the job. The Bible is very specific on this point. "But to all who *received* him, he gave the right to become children of God" (John 1:12).

Receiving involves admitting our limitations, turning to God from self, and trusting Christ to come into our lives, forgive our sin, and begin making us the men he wants us to be.

When NFL linebacker Greg Brezina made the decision to trust Christ, he had been battling a severe temper and drinking problem that had put quite a strain on his marriage. But then Greg heard Russ Knipp, an Olympic and world record weight lifter, explain how he had worked for years to become the strongest man in the world for his size, but had not found true fulfillment and purpose until he committed his life to Jesus Christ.

Later, in his hotel room just before a game against the Rams, Greg found himself praying. "I said, 'Jesus Christ, if you're out there and you really are who Russ Knipp says you are, show me.' I guess I was kind of arrogant to talk to God like that. But I was tired of living like I was, and I needed some answers. I asked Christ to be my Lord and Savior. Christ came into my life, took my guilt away, and gave me a sense of peace."

The biggest area of transformation that Greg and Connie Brezina refer to is their marriage. Connie was skeptical when Greg first informed her of his new commitment. "I thought it would be great if it worked," she recalls. "But he'd been through similar things before." Over the next two weeks she noticed several changes. First he read nine books. "He'd never read before. And he stopped swearing and drinking. He seemed a lot happier."

Connie admits she was somewhat bitter because "I thought I was a better Christian, since I'd go to church on Sunday. But I was unhappy. I, too, was searching. I thought there must be more to life than cooking and cleaning house." In November of 1971, she also made a commitment to Christ.

"The biggest thing that happened was that we stopped cutting each other down with sarcastic comments," continues Connie. "And Greg became a lot more considerate of me and what I thought. He started putting me first and including me in his plans. I started to have confidence in him."

"Often we just wouldn't talk to each other," says Greg. "We'd try to kill each other with silence. Then there were times we'd argue—sometimes two or three times a day. I didn't mark on the calendar the last time we had an argument, but it's been better than three years now."

John "Bull" Bramlett, who played both professional baseball and pro football before retiring to go into business, is another man who tried to fill the God-shaped vacuum with "things." John developed quite a reputation as a troublemaker who enjoyed partying more than practicing, and despite some obvious talent (runner-up to Joe Namath as 1966 Rookie of the Year and the Boston Patriots' M.V.P. in 1970) no professional team kept him under contract very long.

"But the peace that I couldn't find in booze, women, or pills, I've found in Jesus Christ," John says. "I see now that I was fighting myself all those years. I never knew what I wanted. The trophies, the applause, the pats on the back were nice. But ... after all the trophies and all the applause, what did I have? Nothing.

"Somehow God brought me through all those years, and he kept my wife and children home when it would have been so easy for them to leave. Because of the way I had been acting, our marriage was in terrible shape. But together my wife and I are discovering that you don't know love until you have God's love."

What are *you* doing with your spiritual dimension?

Do you find yourself substituting *things* for God? Or relying on "religious" rules and activities?

Or are you becoming *all you can be* by letting Christ fill you with his love and guidance?

Taking that step of commitment and trust—perhaps by a simple, sincere prayer like those of William Jones or Greg

Brezina—is the first key to seeing the impossible take place in your life.

TWO
Let God Do
the Work

I like the illustration that Christ gave of the relationship between the vine and the branch. "I am the true Vine, and my Father is the Gardener," he said in John 15. "Take care to live in me, and let me live in you. For a branch can't produce fruit when severed from the vine."

Practical as always, Christ was drawing his example from a familiar, common sight in Israel: the grapevine. People knew that in order to have a healthy yield of grapes (and eventually, wine) the branch must be firmly embedded in the vine. No branch can produce grapes apart from the vine. The vine is the source of nutrition and power; all the branch has to do is draw that nourishment from the vine. Grapes are the natural by-product of the vine-branch relationship.

And that's exactly how God means for us to succeed in the Total Man life-style. Have you ever seen a branch struggling and *str-a-i-n-i-n-g* to bear fruit? Of course not.

The "fruit of the Spirit"—our Ultimate New Year's Resolution list—is the *natural by-product* of a life focused on Jesus Christ. He does the work of transformation. "Apart from me," Christ said, "you can do nothing." *Our job,* like the branch, is to continually draw on his riches. The Bible sums up our responsibility in one word: ABIDE.

To grow in your relationship with Christ, abide in him. Draw from his abundant riches. Allow him to reproduce his character in you:

... *by going to him regularly in prayer.* Seek his wisdom and guidance on family, business, and personal matters. Ask him to make you a more loving person today. Nothing is too insignificant to talk to God about. And you needn't pray

105

long, formal prayers. If a situation or temptation pops up, send a quick sky telegram like, "Lord, please help me not to get mad, OK?" He will.

... by accepting his continual forgiveness. There'll be many times when you blow it. Resentment, jealousy, lust, an unloving remark, you-name-it. But we're promised, "If we confess our sin, he is faithful and just to forgive us our sin, and to cleanse us from all unrighteousness." To confess is simply to agree with God that an attitude or action is sinful, and that we're truly sorry for it. When the confession is sincere, God's forgiveness is certain.

... by learning from his Word. Someone has aptly called the Bible "God's love letter." You'll not only learn about the attributes of Jesus Christ himself, but all the promises he makes for your personal salvation, guidance, victory over temptation, wisdom, provision for needs. In addition, the Bible is a wealth of practical knowledge in the areas of personal growth, marriage, family, money and time management, business principles, leadership, personal relationships, working relationships, etc.

... by enjoying Christian fellowship. There's something encouraging about meeting together with friends who share the same quality of life that you do. You'll have opportunity to observe what Christ is doing in their lives, while they can see how you're growing in your own faith. Together, you can share joys and concerns and learn from each other's experiences. This is the function of the church as God intended it to be. Find a church where Christ is honored, where his Word is taught, and where the people enjoy rich personal relationships with him and each other.

... by taking the spiritual initiative at home. Christianity is not a "women and children only" relationship, yet that's how we men have been treating it. Mom pulls out the family Bible. Mom jabs Pop in the side when it's time to say grace, or more likely says it herself. Mom prays for the children. Mom makes sure everyone gets to church on time. *Where's Pop?* It's time we men began harnessing the power of Christ's Spirit in our families—perhaps then the home situ-

ation wouldn't be nearly as tragic as it is today.

As you draw on God's power by "abiding in the Vine," you let him do the work. You'll be able to see the gradual transformation taking place. Love will begin to come more naturally. Joy will enliven your home. Peace, patience, kindness, goodness, faithfulness, gentleness, and self-control will become more and more a part of you. You'll be able to affirm with all confidence, "I can do all things through Christ who strengthens me."

As God has done in my own personal life, in my marriage to Kathy, and in the lives of William Jones, Greg Brezina, John Bramlett, and thousands of others, *he will bring out the best in you.* "You will know the truth," as he promises, "and the truth will set you free."

10 A Formula for Personal Problem Solving

...the honey from the comb is sweet to your taste; Know that wisdom is thus for your soul; If you find it, then there will be a future, And your hope will not be cut off.
SOLOMON, Proverbs 24:13, 14

Situation # 1: In the past few months, you've sensed that you and your children seem to be "drifting apart." Your job, combined with their activities, leaves you little time together—and then it's usually for a hurried meal or a half-hour of TV time. What can be done to bring the family back together again?

Situation #2: At last! You have the opportunity to buy the kind of house you and your wife have always wanted. It's *perfect.* But is all that space plus a den and workshop worth an additional $100 a month in payments? Should you—on faith and Great American Determination—go ahead with the deal?

Situation #3: Your parents have invited you and your family to their home for Christmas. Your wife's folks have invited you to *their* place for the same holiday. You visited her folks last Christmas, but yours live so far away that you can't really afford to go now. What do you do?

THE TOTAL MAN

Perhaps you've faced similar situations recently. Maybe some much tougher ones. But in the man's world of personal endeavor, husbanding, fatherhood, financial strategy, in-law politics, and the host of other situations that come along, the responsibility of decision-making and problem-solving can be awesome.

How *can* you work out better-quality time with the children when everyone's schedules are so diverse? Where *is* that fine line between faith and foolishness when it comes to a big financial decision? What's the *best* way to handle those delicate "family folk" situations in which intentions are honorable but feelings can easily be hurt?

The way we go about such decisions can have dramatic effect on ourselves and our families. A misunderstanding could hamper or shatter an important relationship. One financial mistake could wipe out cash reserves or tie up future earnings for years. Your wife and children might have to spend the next decade paying for a poor decision on your part—or for no decision at all.

Problems. Questions. Decisions. Whether we like it or not, they're an inescapable part of the man's world.

And they call for the keenest sense of wisdom we can muster.

Wisdom. I used to be skeptical about this word. Somehow—perhaps from society's stereotype—I had learned to regard a *wise person* as a white-haired sage who had a witty saying for every occasion. We talk about "wise old Ben Franklin" or a "wise old grandfather."

It never even crossed my mind that *I* could obtain wisdom, especially before age sixty-five. I thought that you're born with it, or else it suddenly strikes you someday while you're rocking away on the front porch. And obviously, I didn't fit either category.

So, to be a success, I went after *knowledge* with a passion. Passed all the exams ... well, *most* of 'em. Garnered all the good grades I could. Behaved just enough to maintain a good record in my cumulative file. In my youthful society, being "smart" had more appeal than being "wise" anyway.

I'm not even sure I fooled anyone in that department. But I wasn't long out of school before realizing something: Education had given me all kinds of knowledge, but life demanded much more of me than the facts and figures I'd worked so hard for. Life's problems go far beyond who won the Battle of Bunker Hill or the difference between subject and predicate.

Life's problems demand wisdom.

Every time I found myself asking, "What's the best thing to do in this situation?" I needed to be *wise,* not just smart.

I needed to know how to apply my knowledge in order to make the best possible decisions. I needed deeper insight into the problems I faced, and a sound method for thinking them through.

And therein lies the definition of wisdom.

Wisdom Is More Than Knowledge

The Proverbs, most of which were written by Solomon, could well be called "The Success Philosophy of Earth's Wisest and Richest Ruler." If you ever want the short course in success, read Proverbs. Here, Solomon almost always accompanies the word *wisdom* with three distinct attributes: *knowledge, understanding,* and *discretion* (or *discernment)*.

Let's think about these for a moment. Together, they provide the teamwork of which wisdom is made.

Knowledge is the mind's filing system—the manipulation of information. It's the facts and figures we've learned through schooling, reading, conversations, radio and television. Knowledge is essential to wisdom, but *it is not sufficient in itself.* If one strives for knowledge only, he is like a computer bank with the computer switched off. Without some kind of evaluation process going on, the knowledge will only lie useless.

Understanding is the process of the mind evaluating

111

knowledge. Usually, the facts are weighed in light of personal experience, personal values, or the observed experiences of others. Understanding asks, "What will happen if we choose this option?" and replies as honestly and objectively as possible.

Discretion is the moment of decision—the action phase of wisdom. Discretion is the ability to make the best choice from among two or more alternatives, based on our evaluation *(understanding)* of the strengths and weaknesses of each option.

Whether we realize it or not, we actually go through this three-stage process whenever we're called upon to make a decision. To illustrate, let's assume you need to go to town, and you're trying to decide whether to drive or walk. The process might go something like this:

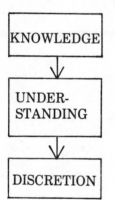

I have to go to town. Town is five miles away. I can drive. Or I can walk.

But five miles is five miles! Walking would take me three or more hours round-trip. Driving might take 15-30 minutes. I don't have three hours.

I will take the car.

In this somewhat oversimplified example, we can see how important each stage of the decision-making process is to the next phase. Without the proper facts *(knowledge)* your evaluation of the facts *(understanding)* would not have been able to compare driving time with walking time. If you had left out the *understanding* stage, you might have taken off on a three-hour hike with only thirty minutes in which to do it. And without the moment of decision *(discretion)* you'd still be standing there wondering what to do.

"But," someone may ask, "what about all the 'split-second' decisions we must make in life? We don't always have *time* to make out a pro and con list in our minds!" True. Fortunately, the human mind thinks faster than we *think* it can. In those split-second crisis situations, the mind *subconsciously* draws on personal experience, personal values, or the observed experiences of others. For example, put yourself in this person's dubious place:

KNOWLEDGE	Joe has just thrown a pie. It's about two feet from my face. I can stand still. Or I can duck.

Consciously, we may think that this is sufficient data to bring about a decision to duck. But subconsciously, in a flash, more wheels are turning:

UNDER-STANDING	When they threw pies on television, everyone's face was a mess. I don't want my face to be a mess (at least, not more than it already is).

The simple knowledge of something flying at you is not enough to cause you to duck. It's the *evaluation of that knowledge* ("flying missiles can hurt; pies are messy") that strikes sufficient fear to bring about the completion of the split-second process:

DISCRETION	Duck!

Again, without all three attributes working together in their proper sequence, a wise decision could not have taken place. If you had misread the facts, misunderstood them, or neglected to make a decision, you'd be spending the next ten minutes wiping pie from your face.

Wisdom happens when all three stages are employed at "peak efficiency." *Maximum knowledge* of the situation, its related facts, its options. *Thorough evaluation* of that knowledge. *A firm decision,* based on the evaluation. Like a chain, the process can only be as strong as its weakest link.

Which leaves lots of room for human error.

Yes, we need to take in all the knowledge we can through education, books, interaction with others, the Bible. And we have a responsibility to set things down and analyze them through the best of human logic. But quite often even those resources are not enough to steer our minds to the right conclusion.

As we pointed out in the last chapter: *We've got to recognize our limitations.* The possibilities of making a decision on insufficient knowledge or inadequate understanding are just too enormous when you consider the complexity of today's problems.

The Solid Starting Point

Solomon in all his wisdom recognized that even *he* needed a solid, inerrant starting point from which to begin every fact-evaluation-decision process. Not as a substitute for human logic and reasoning, but as an *enhancer* of it.

And he wasted no time in identifying that starting point. On the very first page of his book of Proverbs he wrote:

> "I want to make the simple-minded wise!... [and] I want those already wise to become the wiser and become leaders by exploring the depths of meaning in these nuggets of truth." How does a man become wise? The first step is to trust and reverence the Lord! (Proverbs 1:4-9, TLB).

Trust and reverence the Lord. That takes us right back to

114

the last two chapters. When you're living under God's daily guidance, you can add *wisdom* to that list of Ultimate New Year's Resolutions.

Never think for a moment that God is miserly with his wisdom—he actually *wants* you to have it. Do you remember how Solomon became wise?

Shortly after he inherited the throne of Israel from his father David, the Lord appeared to Solomon in a dream. "Ask for anything you want," God said, "and it will be yours."

What would you have asked for? ("Well, Lord, I sure like the looks of the Mercedes ...")

Solomon could have asked for a fancier chariot, or prettier women, or world domination—but he didn't. "Give me an understanding mind so that I can govern your people well and know the difference between right and wrong," he said. "For who by himself is able to carry such a heavy responsibility?"

Solomon recognized his limitations.

Each one of us might do well to compare Solomon's task of leadership with the awesome responsibility we hold in the management of our personal lives, our marriages, our families. *"Give me an understanding mind ... for who by himself is able to carry such a heavy responsibility?"*

How did the Lord respond?

> "Because you have asked for wisdom in governing my people, and haven't asked for a long life or riches for yourself, or the defeat of your enemies—yes, I'll give you what you asked for! I will give you a wiser mind than anyone else has ever had or ever will have! And I will also give you what you didn't ask for—riches and honor!" (1 Kings 3:10-13, TLB).

Solomon woke up thinking that the entire interview was "just a dream." But soon afterward he made his famous decision in the world's most publicized child-custody case. And "word of the king's decision spread quickly throughout the entire nation," the account tells us. "The people were awed as they realized the great wisdom God had given him" (1 Kings 3:28, TLB).

God *wants* to give us wisdom. From James' very straightforward New Testament letter: "If any of you lacks wisdom, let him ask of God, who gives to all men generously and without reproach, and it will be given to him" (James 1:5).

There's only one catch to that promise: James is writing to those who have entrusted their lives to God through Jesus Christ. If you've done so, then you have access to God's wisdom. If you haven't yet, you're on your own, brother.

Solomon exemplified that the starting point of all wisdom is trust and reverence for the Lord. Throughout his life, we can see the direct effect on his decision making: Whenever Solomon put God first in his life, his subsequent *knowledge → understanding → discretion* process yielded wise decisions. But if he ever skipped over the Lord and went directly to the process, his human limitations yielded poor choices for which the entire nation of Israel had to suffer. That's why he wrote, "... don't ever trust yourself. In everything you do, put God first, and he will direct you and crown your efforts with success" (Proverbs 3:5, 6, TLB).

So, from the life experience of the earth's wisest ruler, we have the formula for success in problem solving. See diagram on page 117.

After studying the diagram, let's see how practical the formula can be in solving today's problems. We might not have two young women come to us haggling over which one is the child's true mother, but what about some of these:

"Can we afford a new car now? And if so, which one?"

"What kinds of rules do we need to enforce with our teenage children?"

"Is now the time for a career switch? If so, what's the best field for me to get into?"

"How can we solve our family money problems?"

(What's on your mind right now? Name it.) _____

_____

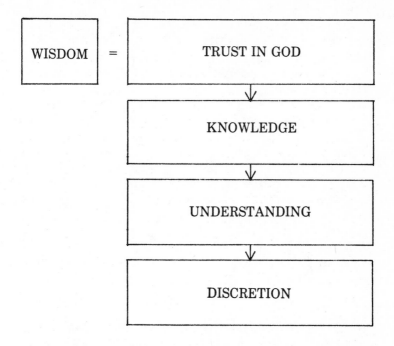

State the problem you're facing as clearly as you can. Then begin to adapt Solomon's formula to your situation by focusing for a few moments on the important starting point.

1. TRUST AND REVERENCE OF THE LORD

The natural tendency we all have is to *reverse* the problem-solving process and place God at the very end. We'll wrestle the problem through and then ask God to bless our plans. Or, if it becomes evident that we really blew our decision, we'll go running to him to bail us out.

We'd save ourselves a bundle of trouble if we'd follow Solomon's advice to *begin at the starting point*. Go to God *first*, not after. His Word may already have the an-

117

swer we need, spelled out for us in black and white.

Or, God may use the direct communication route. As soon as we've stated the problem and asked him for wisdom, he may impress our minds with just the right choice (and make all the other options look comparatively ridiculous).

Or, God just might want us to exercise the minds he's given us. That's where Solomon's formula for personal problem solving comes in.

Begin by thanking God for the problem. While it may cause some pains now, God will use it to help you grow into a wiser, better person. That's why the Bible says, "In everything give thanks." Because "all things work together for good to those who love God."

Then, ask for the Lord's guidance—that he would clear your mind of all misleading thoughts, tangents, or temptations to settle for less than the best.

2. KNOWLEDGE

If necessary, restate your problem so that its wording doesn't limit your creativity. For example, if your problem reads, "How can I get my in-laws off my back?" try rewording it like this: "How can I improve my relationship with my in-laws?" This will allow for a more positive, wider range of options.

When the situation is stated constructively, then you're ready to begin listing all possible courses of action. This, incidentally, can be a valuable experience as a husband and wife team or even as an entire family, provided that the subject matter is suitable for the children. Whenever possible, involve your wife and kids in the process of family problem solving. It's a great tool for communication and caring together.

One popular method of listing options is called "brainstorming." In this method everyone is free to call out any idea that pops up in his mind, no matter how ridiculous it sounds. Every idea is listed on a sheet of paper. For brainstorming to work, four rules must be followed:

1. No criticism or evaluation is allowed yet. Comments such as "Nawww..." or "That would never work!" tend to discourage the free flow of ideas and are therefore verboten.

2. People can call out the wildest ideas as well as the mildest ones. Often, an outlandish solution can later be modified into just the right choice.

3. For the moment, go for quantity, not quality. When many options are listed, chances of coming upon the best one are increased.

4. Everyone is encouraged to build upon each other's ideas. One person's laughing joke of a solution might spawn a realistic idea in another person's mind.

When you feel that you've listed all possible options, and that you've gathered all the facts necessary to evaluate the problem objectively, then you're ready for stage three.

3. UNDER-STANDING

Now's the time to be honest with each other about every possible solution you've

119

listed. Some can probably be junked right away. The others, though, you will want to weigh carefully in light of some serious evaluation questions:

1. Is this option a violation of God's Word?

2. Is it a violation of man's civil law?

3. Is this choice in line with my/our personal priorities?

4. Would this solution hurt someone else?

5. What will be the long-range effect of this choice? (Place yourself at age seventy-five, looking back on life. Are you glad you made the decision you did? If not, what went wrong?)

6. Do the advantages outweigh the disadvantages? (Make a Pro-Con list for each option. Under "Pro," list every advantage you can think of; under "Con," every disadvantage. Which side outweighs the other?)

These questions, and any others that weigh heavily on your mind, will help you narrow down your list of alternatives to the most viable ones. Then comes the most important moment in the entire process.

4. DISCRETION

After weighing all the facts, and perhaps sleeping and thinking on them, make your decision. Choose the course(s) of action that stand up best to your evaluation questions. Then begin putting your solution(s) into action.

120

Look on Problems
as Opportunities

No human being will ever be free from problems, regardless of how much wisdom he attains. There seems to be an uncanny ring of truth to that little rule called Murphy's Law: "If anything can possibly go wrong, it will!"

For obvious reasons, Kathy and I were once toying with the idea of naming our ten-year-old Plymouth "Murphy." In the early days of our marriage, it seemed that just when we had the least amount of money and the most errands to run, that car would start making the most cantankerous noises. It meant $140 here, $77.98 there. Two, maybe three days in the shop each time.

Soon it was evident that we had a decision to make. Not to get a new car—that was out of the question for at least a couple of years. The choice we needed to make was one of *attitude*. Were we going to complain, worry, and shake our fists at fate for its lousy sense of timing? Let *things* get us upset and irritable with each other?

Or would we relax—and look for something positive in the experience?

The second alternative looked a lot more difficult, given man's penchant for the negative. But we knew that, if the Plymouth was any indicator of how we would someday respond to *deeper* problems, then our health, outlook, and marriage relationship could end up in a pile of frayed nerves.

That's when we remembered a maxim written awhile back by a man named Henry J. Kaiser. "Problems," Kaiser wrote, "are only opportunities in work clothes."

Opportunities? Is a $140 repair bill an *opportunity?*

Kathy and I began thinking about that one. We had to keep shoving away the negative feelings that had clung to us for so long. But gradually, we *could* see some positive things about the way our car had taken it upon itself to personally prove the validity of Murphy's Law.

121

For one thing, I was learning more about the mechanics of a car—some important knowledge I'd failed to go after in my growing-up years.

For another, we were learning how to budget wisely. Even though we were on a limited salary, those repair bills never kept adequate food from our table.

Then, the days without wheels were teaching Kathy and me to be flexible in our errands with the car. Instead of running to town every other day for one or two items, we started making a list of things-to-do that could all be done in one trip at the end of the week.

And, hard as it is to admit, even a senile Plymouth in love with the lube rack taught us faithfulness to God. Seems that that car *knew* when we weren't trusting God daily as we should. Every time things would go plooey and the money situation looked impossible, our route was predictable: Right back to the Lord, telling him about our needs. *God will sometimes allow problems to happen in order for us to learn to trust him more faithfully.*

Problems are only opportunities in work clothes. *Every* problem has a lesson for us.

So when you're facing a tough situation, eliminate the negative. Agree with your wife and family that you'll try to look on every problem as an opportunity to learn or grow. Make it a point to ask, "What does God want to teach us?" And never allow yourself or anyone to sigh, "Oh, if only ..." Negativism is the biggest hindrance to the decision-making process.

Here's a simple way to launch that new outlook: Make a deal with your family that you'll all try to wipe the word "problem" from your vocabulary. Instead, substitute the word, "opportunity." Or, "situation." Or, "test." Positive words. They call us into *action,* not defeat.

Kathy and I have found that looking for the *good* in every situation has made a world of difference in the attitude of our home. We've been able to relax and enjoy ourselves more—even during tense times—simply through faith that

God is in the process of teaching us something. And most important, looking for the *good* frees us from negative attitudes which can cripple our minds during the problem-solving process.

But then, we no longer have problems at our house.

We have opportunities.

Section Two

THE LIBERATED HUSBAND

11
What Does a Woman Need?

Woman was created from the rib of man. She was not made from his head–to top him, nor from his feet–to be trampled on. She was made from his side–to be equal to him, from under his arm–to be protected by him, from near his heart to be loved by him.
AUTHOR UNKNOWN

Eliza Doolittle was driving Professor Henry Higgins and Colonel Pickering up the wall. They had made a wager that they could turn this ragamuffin flower girl into a specimen of eloquence and beauty—a logical, objective, and scientific undertaking. But they hadn't taken into account Eliza's resentment at being a guinea pig. She couldn't remain passive and objective—not when her feelings were at stake.

So in this scene from *My Fair Lady*, we hear Higgins and Pickering lamenting to each other how impossible it is to figure out women. "Why can't a woman be more like a man?" they ask. Then she would be understandable, less emotional, easier to get along with.

To figure out the woman is a task most men have deemed improbable. I know more than one husband who has vowed to write a book entitled, "Everything I Understand About My Wife"—its pages would be entirely blank. There is a mys-

127

tique about the female which men have been trying for centuries to ascertain, a sort of predictable unpredictability that can make marriage either fascinating or frustrating. Fascinating, if we as husbands recognize the fact that there *are* differences in the emotional makeup of man and woman, and give her the freedom to be herself. Frustrating, if we refuse to allow for such differences, letting her expression of emotional needs touch off marital fireworks.

Why can't a woman be more like a man? It would be a terribly dull world if she were! It is generally thought that the male is moved by reason, logic, and objectivity while the female tends to be more subjective. Of course, there are many exceptions to this and I do *not* mean that man is incapable of emotion, or that woman is incapable of logic. Rather, woman has been given a priceless sensitivity for experiencing the deep feelings of life that we often miss.

That sensitivity has proven a complement to my cold rationality over and over. I might say, "I think we ought to do such and such," confident that I've made the most prudent choice. But Kathy might see it from a different, more significant point of view. "But if we did that," she'll suggest, "don't you think it might hurt So-and-so's feelings?" Fact is, I never even thought of So-and-so's feelings. So we discuss the matter further, and come up with a far better solution. Her warm spirit has softened my cold rationality. We make a good team.

Kathy's unique emotional makeup, I've discovered, is crucial to the success of our marriage. Understanding her needs will help me to step out of my personal shell and to care—*really care*—about her fulfillment as a woman. It makes me a far less selfish individual, and brings us the mutual joy of experiencing the ultimate in a husband/wife relationship.

One of the best projects we've ever done was to sit down over a cup of coffee and talk about the emotional needs we each have. We made lists, asked questions. As we talked, it occurred to me that I was virtually ignorant of the things that are really important to a woman. I had not taken the time to understand Kathy's uniqueness because I had been

128

expecting her to think and feel the same way I did. As a result, I was cheating her out of her unique contribution to our marriage, squelching her as she tried to become a maximum woman.

That evening launched me on a project that eventually became the basis for this book. I began interviewing wives about the needs of a woman, trying to gather a basic list that I could share with husbands. Most wives itemized the same needs, confirming my suspicion that the list is almost universal.

On hearing that I was considering putting my findings into a book for husbands, one wife pleaded, "Oh, please *do*. I know *so* many women who are frustrated because their husbands just don't make an effort to understand them. And we *are* different—they need to know that."

For those husbands, and for you and me, here's what we discovered.

The need for security.
Man has a penchant for daring, dreaming, and risk-taking. He thinks often of improving his lot, or trying his hand at something completely new, or finding that perfect scheme that will make him richer, stronger, and wiser. For those rewards he is willing to risk a temporary setback or even a major catastrophe—just to know that he tried.

The woman, however, tends to be a conservative when it comes to speculation and grandiose dreams. As her husband shares his ideas, she wonders where the money will come from. She would rather plod along steadily, secure and solvent, than risk the savings account for a new venture. Security is important to her, and she finds that security in you, in her home, in her family, in finances. The husband needs to exercise diligent tenderness whenever he thinks of uprooting the status quo.

The need for love.
All of us need love, but it is the *expression* of that love which distinguishes male from female. Most men are satisfied if

their wives tell them "I love you" once a month. The woman needs to hear it every day.

Said an old Vermont farmer, married over forty years: "I love Sarah Jane so much it's all I can do to keep from telling her." Do tell her! No matter how kind you are to her, or how lavish a gift you get her, your wife's day isn't complete unless she hears "I love you" from an honest heart.

But your words must be consistent with your actions. "I love you" will mean nothing if you then proceed to ridicule her in front of others, or fail to express gentleness in personal communication. She needs to hear it, and then see it in action.

The need to express emotion.

Tears play a healthy role in the life of a woman by soothing tensions and washing away potential bitterness. For this very reason, women are for the most part healthier than men. We have been conditioned to suppress our feelings. They have been encouraged to express them. It's something most women do rather well.

Kathy doesn't need a bawl very often, but when I sense the flood mounting inside her, I try to tactfully encourage it. "Do you need a good cry, honey?" I'll ask. If she indicates yes, I ask, "Do you need to be alone, or do you need for me to hold you?" In a few moments, when everything's fine and relaxed, we talk about the experience. I may have done something to upset her—if so, I want to know about it. Or circumstances may have just built up to the breaking point. In spite of the tears, it's been a good experience in learning more about the intricacies of the woman. Learn to regard her emotions as a friend to the marriage, not a foe.

The need for companionship.

It's important for her to have her women friends and for you to be "good buddies" with the guys. But is *she* your *best* friend? She wants to be. A woman experiences a special exhilaration when she knows her husband would rather be with her than with anyone else. "Let's go for a long walk—just the two of us" is music to her ears. She wants to be a part of what you're thinking and doing. She'd be honored (perhaps flabbergasted) if you wanted to be a part of *her* activities. Smart husbands go out of their way to make their women feel special.

The need for closeness.

Sometimes she'd rather be alone, but far more often she needs your closeness. Mix closeness with tenderness. A hug, a squeeze of the hand, a kiss. Women have a hard time explaining this need, but it is very real to them. One told me, "There are times when I just need for him to *be there,* unhurried. Even if we don't have anything to say. It just assures me that everything's all right."

The need to express herself creatively.

It's a rare woman who doesn't have some latent talent within her that is yearning to be expressed. You can encourage her by helping make sure that the load of routine housework does not stifle her creative abilities. Most women crave the time to sew, read, write, paint, cultivate plants, develop musical talents, experiment with new recipes, or make crafts. Adult education offers a treasury of classes in art, literature, homemaking, or practically any area she may be interested in.

If it's been some time since she tried her hand at anything new, she may have doubts about her creative aptitude. An encouraging nudge from you and continued moral support throughout her endeavor might be all that's needed to get her on her way.

The need to express herself mentally.

I have had the uncomfortable privilege of observing several husbands who thought it unmanly to let their wives contribute to a group discussion. It was funny, yet tragic. Somehow these men had gotten the idea that the woman's role is to sit in silent admiration as their brilliant husbands solve the crises of the world.

We so pride ourselves in our shrewd capacity for reason that we easily forget: Women can think, too. Their minds combined with their hearts can make a potent tool in discernment, often more penetrating than that of their male counterparts. It takes a lot for me to admit that. But I've been listening, for once.

Sure, a woman wants to be respected for her cooking and housewifery, but even more, she covets her husband's respect for her mentality. Here again she needs your encouragement. In discussions, ask her what she thinks on a subject. Then listen as she speaks, instead of waiting for a spot where you can jump back into the conversation. Ask her to tell you about the book she's reading, or about the course she's been taking.

The need for intimacy.

Intimacy is the deeper manifestation of that "closeness" so vital to a woman's sense of well-being. It is the communication of mutual secrets and very private jokes, the sharing of each other's insecure moments without fear of rejection or rebuke, the sexual embraces that signify two becoming one.

Intimacy is so priceless to her because it is just between the two of you. She knows she has you all to herself, that you consider her your special friend and confidante. It makes her feel extra special.

When the close moments look like they'll become intimate ones, let them. She's signaling that she needs you now. Cancel the committee meeting, postpone your evening work, take the phone off the hook, and share.

The need for spiritual fulfillment.

St. Augustine wrote, "Thou hast made us for Thyself, O God, and our hearts are restless until they find their rest in

Thee." God made all of us with a built-in need to trust him, but a woman's need can often be accentuated by her sensitivity to life. While the male might try to "gut it out" before turning a problem over to Christ, the woman will often be driven to him sooner by her feelings. "Let's think it through and then pray about it," I tell Kathy. She'll say, "Why don't we pray about it and *then* think it through?" Her sensitivity has increased her capacity to trust as well as her need for spiritual communication with God.

The best way you can help fulfill your wife's spiritual restlessness is to provide a strong example for her to follow. A woman can trust a husband whom she knows is being led by God. Nothing will give her a greater sense of security than a husband totally committed to living as Christ taught. Study the Bible and pray regularly, *together*. Relax, laugh, and enjoy life, *together*.

You need never be jealous of your wife's intimacy with God, nor she of yours. Why? Because if God is at the center of your relationship, he does not split you apart—*he draws you closer together:*

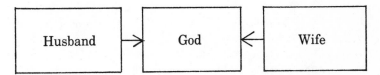

The need for romance.
Romance is all the little things that we'd be embarrassed to have the guys in the bowling league hear about. The flowers you bought her last week, and the week before. The candlelight and music to surround a bucket of fried chicken. The perfume and new nightgown. Taking her for a long walk in lieu of watching "Charlie's Angels." Celebrating all the anniversaries.

For men, love is a process. We've courted her and won her hand—now, on with business. But for her, love is an adventure. Doing things for each other, dreaming up surprises.

Little things. Fun things. Insane things.

Keep letting her know that she's still worth chasing.

The need for communication.

"Much unhappiness has come into the world because of bewilderment and things left unsaid." Dostoyevsky's perceptive statement is particularly *apropos* to marriage, where a silent partnership can prove disastrous.

Among the wives interviewed, an alarming number rated their husbands very low in the art of communication. Some cited competition with the television set (left on during dinner and throughout the evening); others attributed poor communication to fatigue, worry, and the demands of the job. One wife probably cornered the problem when she observed, "I just don't think he *wants* to talk about things on a deep level. We talk about the weather and about the neighbors, but when the conversation shifts to anything more significant, he clams up. Sometimes I have to almost drag a decision or opinion out of him."

After a full day of interacting and decision-making at the office, the husband's tendency is often to withdraw into himself for needed peace and quiet. This is why good communication is such hard work. It requires us to be outgoing when we'd rather be ingrown, to be interested in someone else when we're more concerned with ourselves.

We all need our moments of silence, but watch out: They can be habit-forming because they require so little effort.

Good communication is one of marriage's most unselfish forms of giving. It is intimacy verbalized. As you and your wife seek to become one, communication is the process by which you'll become of one mind.

The need to feel attractive.

Back in my single days, one of my older brothers taught me an important lesson about women. Paul's wife, a beautiful woman who wore glasses, had been expressing an interest in switching to contact lenses. Knowing that Paul was then on a rather limited income, I asked him privately, "Do you really think contact lenses are that important right now?" Paul's reply: "They're important to her, so they're important to me." Period.

He had already gained an insight that I would realize several years later: A woman's desire to be physically attractive far transcends mere vanity. She needs to know that she turns you on.

Why else does a woman spend so much time shopping for clothes, makeup, and accessories; or primping and experimenting with hairstyles; or gazing into the mirror and the bathroom scale? Contrary to popular thought, she is *not* doing it to frustrate an impatient husband. She is doing it to please him, to find that perfect combination which will evoke a genuine "Wow!"

Regardless of what the mirror and scales tell her, you are the indicator she depends on most. If she looks great, tell her so. Then back up your statement with continued flirtations. Your positive words and actions are the best encouragement you can give her to stay fit and beautiful.

"But," some of you are saying, "what if my wife has let herself go? I find it hard to say 'You turn me on' to a woman who could play linebacker for the Rams." Here, the loving husband exercises a blend of sensitivity and positive thinking. Instead of cracking fat jokes at your wife's expense, look for something positive on which to compliment her. Her hairstyle. Her makeup. Her jewelry. If even those are lacking, how about the color of her eyes?

Then invite her to join you in a family fitness routine (that's right—*you* set the example). If she sheds a pound, rejoice with her. If she gains, don't scorn her, but simply say, "We'll get that pound next week."

Your positive attitude can be the key to your wife's attractiveness. One smart husband told me that his wife struggled for months to lose weight, to no avail. Suddenly it dawned on the husband that he had been inadvertently discouraging

135

her, either by his wisecracks or his silence. He determined to try being an encouragement.

One day she tried particularly hard to follow her diet. That evening, as they were undressing, he looked at his wife's thighs. "Honey," he said, "am I just seeing things? I think you're losing weight!"

His wife just beamed. "Really?" she said.

"That's *great,* Honey," he continued. "Keep up the good work!"

She did, and with noticeable results. Simply because her husband knew the value of positive reinforcement.

Never underestimate her need to feel attractive. More than most men realize, it plays a big role in her total outlook.

The need to be encouraged.

Building each other up is one of the most vital foundation blocks of a good marriage. It is an art which, short of insincere flattery, can never be overdone.

When I worked as feature editor for a magazine, I observed time and again how different writers performed under varying conditions. If I simply made an assignment and then waited in repose for the manuscript, the writer often would experience difficulty in motivation, discipline, and in the actual writing. But when I made a point of complimenting a writer on his previous article, and checking regularly with him to see if I could lend some encouragement, the manuscripts would hit my desk on or before the deadline. And usually, they were of much higher quality.

People feel and perform better when they know that others have confidence in their abilities. You've undoubtedly discovered this about yourself, in your own job. A lack of confidence or encouragement can soon stifle you into self-doubt and/or complacency.

At home, your wife is experiencing the exact same need. What is she trying to accomplish? To be the best possible wife? She needs your feedback and encouragement. A job?

WHAT DOES A WOMAN NEED?

Tell her, "I'm proud of you!" To be the best cook she can be?
She needs your compliments on her cuisine. In whatever she
tries to do, let her have no doubt that you believe in her.
"Building her up" is not puffery, but simply giving credit
where credit is due.

The need to be appreciated.

So tightly meshed with encouragement is appreciation. In
strong marriages, the two go hand in hand.

Several wives underscored for me their intense need to
not be taken for granted. "Sometimes he doesn't seem to
notice that the house is clean, the laundry is washed, and
the children are still in one piece," one wife confided. "All I
hear is, 'Has the paper come yet?' and 'When's supper?' "

Alan Lakein, in his book *How to Get Control of Your Time
and Your Life,* has written a brief account which might
wake up several of us who haven't realized what a housewife
goes through:

> A woman is fragmented mentally, emotionally, and
> physically. The demands go on 24 hours a day, and
> deadlines like getting a meal on the table or clothes on
> the family's back are inexorable. Interruptions tend to
> be traumatic—children get hurt, or sick, or need emo-
> tional help RIGHT NOW. So do husbands.
>
> A father is always playing neat, satisfying games dur-
> ing a lot of this. He can give and take orders, move his
> checkers ahead one square a day, and believe his job is
> important—while a mother stays on the scene ALL the
> time, handling inputs from every direction. She can't
> turn off her job at five o'clock and come home to find
> dinner waiting. The truth is that with purchasing,
> budgeting, minor repairs, nutrition, keeping inven-
> tory, deciding how many kids can wear this sweater or
> use that bike—on top of the physical labor of it all, a

137

woman is running a very tough little business in which the responsibility is all hers.

And I thought *my* job was tough!

Saying "thank you" is still a common courtesy in society, but you'd be surprised at how readily it drops out of a marriage. Appreciation is just like love to her: She needs to hear it, then see it in action.

I'm still learning in this department, and to help myself, I try to keep my eyes open for the little things Kathy does around the apartment while I'm at work. Then I thank her, sometimes specifically ("Thank you, Honey, for ironing my shirts so well") and sometimes generally ("I really appreciate you. You're the best wife I could have asked for"). I can put that appreciation into action in a variety of ways. By a special gift or dinner out, for example. By picking up after myself around the apartment. And by actually pitching in and giving her a hand in that endless list of chores.

Edgar Watson Howe wrote, "The greatest humiliation in life is to work hard on something from which you expect great appreciation, and then fail to get it." The homemaker is one of the hardest-working persons in the world. Stay alert for ways to show your appreciation.

The need to be needed.

This is not your need for her skills at housewifery, for when you get right down to it, you *could* hire a maid, a cook, and a nanny. The woman's need to be needed goes much deeper than that. Men don't enjoy it, for the fulfillment of this need usually comes when we are at our weakest.

These are the moments when the husband has reached a point of discouragement or failure, and his own sense of security is beginning to quake beneath him. Perhaps he's had a rotten week on the job, or he's down on himself for a financial mistake. Then, too, the uncertain future might be playing havoc with his mind. Combined with actual physical fatigue, self-doubt makes a miserable man.

138

For too long, the *macho* in us has prevented us from sharing these brief flecks of insecurity with other people, especially our women. Sometimes we'll remain silent to protect them and the kids from fear. In most cases, however, we don't want to give anyone a hint that we've temporarily lost control of a situation. Every day, the "I am the master of my fate" syndrome turns thousands of us into human pressure cookers.

This is where you need your partner, and she yearns for your need. She does not consider it unmasculine of you to confess that you are frustrated or frightened. She wants to encourage you, to hold you, to assure you that no matter what happens, her love for you won't be dented in the slightest.

When you need her in those moments, don't hold back. She is your partner during the bad times as well as the good. And you'll be doing yourself and your marriage a healthy favor.

"I-just-don't-know-what-I-need!"

This is when she needs you most of all, though she may not want you around. If that sounds confusing, it's because circumstances, emotions, bodily changes, and even the weather are all combining to confuse her. She's not quite sure of herself, or of you, at the moment.

Wives who listed this need were at a loss to explain it adequately, though most underscored it as crucial. As one informed me, "Sometimes I feel jittery and depressed at the same time. I'm afraid, yet I don't care about much of anything. I guess this feeling makes me the most insecure because I can never really put my finger on it."

Kathy also brought up this uncertainty when we were discussing her personal needs. When I asked her how she wanted me to respond when she goes through the rough moments, she replied, "More than anything, be patient with me ... and realize that I don't *want* to be that way. It's a temporary thing, and if I snap your head off or act unloving,

139

it's my insecurity—not the real me—showing through.

"Then," Kathy continued, "I need for you to be available, but not hovering. I want to know that you're there and that everything's all right."

"Do you want me to hold you?" I asked.

"Maybe, but not always," Kathy replied. "I think the woman needs to decide that, instead of the man smothering her. She may want to be left alone for a while, until she gets her head straightened out."

Kathy's insights were good for me to hear. Early in our marriage, when the moody moments would hit her, I took them as a personal affront. If Kathy was morose, I assumed she was angry with me over who-knows-what-this-time? I responded with real anger. Which only compounded her frustration.

When your woman is in the "I-don't-know-what-I-need" mood, resist the temptation to anger. She needs your patience now more than ever. You might want to assure her, "I'm here whenever you want to talk about it." Above all, give her the time she needs to sort things out.

In looking back over the uniqueness of the married woman, one thing becomes evident: Most of her needs involve her husband. That is why we men can no longer afford to assign higher importance to our jobs or activities than to our own wives. If we do, we are cheating on them—failing to meet the basic needs inherent in a love relationship.

In marriage, there is an enemy of love far greater than hate. That enemy is *self*. It stands as a roadblock to all these expressions of love when we allow the "what's-in-it-for-me?" attitude, or just plain laziness, to dominate our personal lives.

Which points us to one of the most important keys to mutual fulfillment in marriage: *giving*. Considering her basic needs more important than our selfish desires. And the spirit of continual giving—of our time, our selves, our understanding—requires an unabashed brand of love.

We'll explore the nature of that love in the next chapter.

12 Who's in Charge?

In spite of its fantasies and weaknesses, television reveals a lot about contemporary thinking.

Take society's view of the family man. "Little House on the Prairie" looks back into the nineteenth century, where Charles Ingalls is an honest, sincere, hard-working farmer. No matter how tough Ingalls's day is, he always takes the time to love, talk, and play with his children. Mrs. Ingalls submits lovingly to Charles' leadership—not because he lords it over her, but out of a genuine respect for her husband. Charles Ingalls seems to relish his wife's input as he contemplates a decision, yet they both know that the decision is his. There is harmony in the Ingallses' household.

"The Waltons" moves us ahead several decades to the mid-30s. In this program the spotlight is primarily on the children, but we begin to see a changing view of the father image. John Walton works hard in his family lumber business to make ends

141

meet during the depression, and there is no doubt about his love and loyalty to his family. There is often some question, however, about who exactly is in charge in his family. Walton's authority is sometimes usurped by his wife and even by Grandma Walton. In one episode, for example, John-Boy (their eldest son, striving to become a writer) was about to sign a contract to have his first book published. "Don't you think you ought to read it first, son?" Mr. Walton suggested, to which his wife replied, "Oh, John, let him go ahead." John let his son proceed, only to discover later that the contract was for a vanity publishing firm—to which an author must pay a handsome sum in order to see his book published. Walton, although trying his best to be a good husband and father, will sometimes sit in the background while his wife or mother makes the family rules and decisions.

"Happy Days," a nostalgia-inspired comedy set in the late '50s, depicts the contemporary dad as a somewhat rotund, henpecked man who sits in the living room with his paper and pipe after a hard day at the office. "Mr. C" is usually the straight man for the family jokes, the fall-guy for Richie and Fonzie's escapades, and a generally frustrated man who can never seem to get on top of a situation. Whenever he does display some authority to either his wife, son, or daughter, he is usually talked or conned out of it.

Commercials of the '70s have further emasculated men to the point where more than one commercial has the man whining, "I'm going home to mother." A little pipsqueak with coke bottle glasses and 1940s bow tie tells us about his problems with diarrhea. In the numerous husband-wife commercials, the husband is often the dummy to whom the wife must explain, over and over, the virtues of Brand X over Brand Y.

If television doesn't *form* the thinking of a nation, it certainly *reveals* it. Our nation is going through an identity crisis in marital leadership, a crisis in which we see several different attitudes taking place:

1. The husband is The Leader, and that means *"Fall in!* There will be no dissention, no disagreement, no 'doing your

own thing' while I'm in charge. You're here, wife, to serve me and raise the kids."

2. The husband is trying to assert himself as leader, but his wife won't tolerate it. There was no agreement at the beginning of the marriage regarding the chain of command in the household. The husband has acted weakly, or not at all. Now, we hear the husband saying, "I *will* be the boss of this house, and I will *not* come out from under this bed!"

3. Both spouses have agreed that the husband is responsible for family leadership, but not for family dictatorship. He realizes the value of his wife's mentality and experiences, and feels it only wise to get maximum input from her before making a final decision. They work together as a team of "equals"—but realize that every team, for the sake of avoiding chaos, needs a captain.

4. The husband and wife live together in a sort of no-leader coexistence. This is a fairly recent occurrence, a more militant outgrowth of the feminist movement. Anthropologists, zoologists, and sociologists will tell us that in any given group of human beings or animals, a leader will soon emerge through either election or power struggle. Living creatures *need* a chain of command to exist in a group. For the modern, "liberated" husband and wife to agree to a leaderless coexistence is to agree to a life of frustration in which there is no established procedure for resolving problems.

5. The wife is the leader, usually taking over the responsibility because her husband has failed to lead during the early years of marriage. It happens when the husband prefers being silent to communicating openly; his noncommittal attitude, when the young wife eagerly waits for him to assert himself, prompts her to begin doing the talking, then the thinking, for the family. Our society calls him the "henpecked husband" and her the "domineering wife." It's happened in more homes than husbands would care to admit.

From this confusion, it is obvious that a basic principle of leadership is needed for the home to be happy. It must be a principle which demeans no one, which provides for open discussion and even dissenting opinions, yet allows for an efficient system of goal-setting and decision-making.

God created marriage knowing that any grouping of two or more people needs such a principle of leadership. He wants marriages to work. And in Ephesians 5:21-25 (TLB) he has prescribed the principle for us to follow:

> Honor Christ by submitting to each other. You wives must submit to your husbands' leadership in the same way you submit to the Lord. For a husband is in charge of his wife in the same way Christ is in charge of his body the church (He gave his very life to take care of it and be its Savior!) ... And you husbands, show the same kind of love to your wives as Christ showed to the church when he died for her.

Here, God has made it quite clear that he has given you, the husband, *responsibility for leadership* in your marriage. *I* didn't say it. Masters and Johnson didn't say it. *God* said it! It is your duty to "take charge"—to maintain a home atmosphere where your wife and children have no question of who is watching out for them. You are responsible for the mood and direction of the household. But God has qualified that ordination with two other important stipulations.

The first is to *submit to each other*. The verse later speaks of a wife submitting to her husband's authority, but take note: *this command is for the husband as well.*

Mutual submission does not mean "let thyself become henpecked." It is simply each spouse saying, "Up to now, as a single person, I have been naturally self-centered. But now we are two becoming one. So I yield to you my right to selfishness. Instead of *me*, from now on it is *we*. Partners. Best friends. Confidantes."

As the husband and wife grow together in unity of body, mind, and spirit, agreement on procedures and decisions becomes more and more natural because their two sets of values are being molded into one. But *impasses* will happen, and to prevent chaos or stalemate a decision must be made.

144

As designated leader, you are responsible for that final decision.

But remember, too, that mutual submission does not entitle you to lord it over her. It is instead an assurance that God created man and woman as *equal* in personhood, different only in the responsibilities they are to fulfill. This does *not* exclude the wife from the decision-making process. In fact, it is your responsibility to encourage, seek out, and listen to her viewpoint, evaluate it objectively, and then decide in favor of her opinion if she indeed shows the greater wisdom.

Which tends to bother us a little, doesn't it? As a man, I pride myself on being rational, and when I make a decision I want it to be the right one. But frequently when I'm just about to decide, Kathy comes up with something entirely different—a woman's point of view. Sometimes it's nothing more than an intuition. But deep down, I know that she may be right. Her opinion might in this case be a wiser one than mine. And it bugs me.

I'm bothered because Kathy's exercise of her mental wisdom challenges my leadership. Shouldn't I be making the decisions around here?

This is where "submit to each other" comes in.

I am *responsible* for the decision made, but that does not allow for despotism on my part. The fact is, I would be stupid not to recognize that God gave Kathy a brain. She can think and reason, too—in some areas, more clearly than I can. It would be wasteful not to utilize her thinking as we contemplate a goal, a budgetary decision, or even one of marriage's necessary little disagreements.

So it needn't threaten me at all. I'm learning now to be thankful for Kathy's input. God has given her to me to complete the team of home leadership. If I'm smart, I recognize her opinion not as a threat to my decision-making ability, but as a complement to it.

Submitting to each other can also employ the tool of *delegation*. I may not be present to make a decision, or there could be several areas in which my wife is far more qualified than I. Last month, for example, Kathy needed a new steam iron. Now she was a Home Economics minor in college, and the closest I ever get to an iron is to loft a golf ball onto the green. So instead of my deciding which iron to buy, I delegated the decision to her. Of course, she chose a good one. But it would look awfully funny in my golf bag. Likewise, when I'm out of town, or busy on a project, I'll delegate certain financial and household decisions for Kathy to handle. She enjoys the challenge, and her wisdom hasn't ever disappointed me.

Marriage is actually a partnership among equals in which God seems to have intended a president/vice president relationship between husband and wife. A company vice president is no less a *person* than the company president. The only difference is in their responsibilities. Each is equally vital to the success of the company. A shrewd president will in fact maintain close communication with his vice president, consulting on decisions to be made, taking the initiative to work out problems and differences, forming policy together, even delegating decisions and responsibilities.

The second condition under which God gave us leadership responsibility is *love*. In marriage the two are inseparable. Love without leadership can result in chaos. And leadership without love can result in tyranny.

And as in everything else, the Creator of marriage has provided a perfect example of the kind of love that works:

"And you husbands, show the same kind of love to your wives as Christ showed to the church when he died for her."

"The church" means you and me. Just as Christ loves us, so we are to love our wives.

We may or may not have that euphoric, ooey-gooey feeling that the world has termed "love." We may be good providers, good at giving gifts and taking her out to dinner, or good sex partners. But where we often hit a snag is in giving of *ourselves*. It's hard. It's contrary to our selfish human nature. But it's what our wives need the most.

What is Christlike love?

His life shows us several key attributes:

146

1. *Love is unconditional.* "No ifs, ands, or buts about it, I love you!" Do we *deserve* Christ's love? Never! But he loves us just the same, and nothing will ever change or weaken that love.

Perhaps you've heard of the three major types of love. The first is *eros* or sensuous love. For this reason alone many couples enter into marriage, only to lose their attraction for one another and discover that "we don't love each other any more." The second is *phileo,* the love of friendship. *Phileo* is a tremendous asset to marriage, for the husband and wife should be best friends to each other. But *phileo* is still an insufficient bond for permanence. There are simply too many times in marriage when you don't feel friendly to your spouse. In argument, disagreement, or during the inevitable moods, something else is needed or the marriage bond can wear thin.

That's where *agape* comes in. *Agape* is a term introduced by Christ himself which means "I love you although I may disagree with you. I love you in spite of any unattractiveness, arguments, or moods. Nothing you do will change the fact that I love you." Without the motivating Spirit of Christ inside you, you're capable of mustering only a cheap imitation of *agape* love. The real thing is nothing short of permanent, weathering storms of argument, tragedy, loss of physical appeal, sexual temptation. *Agape* lasts because it seeks the best for the other person.

Marriage as God designed it is a beautiful combination of all three types of love, but *agape* is what holds it all together. Love in spite of. Unconditional.

2. *Love is sacrificial.* Yes, Christ died for us, and a true man will protect his loved ones with his own life—but Christ also gave of something much more common. His time.

Does my use of time show my wife that I love her more than my job, my hobby, or things-I-just-gotta-do? A man once told me that he could never figure out why his wife always seemed to need that long hug, that extra assurance of his love, just when he was rushing out the door in a big hurry. "When my schedule is free, she'll always keep herself busy," he said. "But whenever I'm in a hurry to go somewhere or accomplish a job, she seems to hang to me. I feel awful leaving her."

"You can count on it," I told him. "Because as long as you act as though you don't have time for her, she'll wonder how important she is to you."

Sacrificial love *makes the time* for the important things when there are often much more "urgent" things to do. It is inherent in *agape* love, for it puts her needs before your own.

3. *Love is acting like a servant.* "What?" I hear some of you saying. "A servant to my wife?"

Not in a Royal Guard sense. Let's look at Christ for a moment. One day, confident in his power and leadership, Jesus Christ humbly stooped down to wash his disciples' feet—a custom of comfort and hygiene after a long, dusty trip. Christ's disciples objected when he did this, for they considered it a job too lowly for him. But his purpose was to back up a claim he had made earlier: "Anyone wanting to be a leader among you must be your servant." In other words, he who really cares about the needs of people, and takes action to meet those needs, is best qualified to be a leader.

Men of the Archie Bunker variety expect to have the beer and paper rushed to them by a doting Edith as they sit in their overstuffed thrones. Christ turned the tables on that concept. A true family leader is the man confident enough in his masculinity to pitch in when he can and help make his wife's job easier.

And the amazing thing is, helping her out like that doesn't spoil her concept of you one bit. It's just another indication that you think she's worth it all.

4. *Love is being a spiritual leader.* Christ's ultimate objective while on earth was to show us a liberating way to know God personally and have eternal life after physical death. So he was above all a spiritual leader, teaching and guiding his men in the truth that the abundant life is the Christ-centered life.

Our task of loving is incomplete, men, if we fail our wives in this area. And unfortunately, this is where a lot of us have been the biggest duds.

First Corinthians 11:3 (TLB) tells us that "... a wife is responsible to her husband, her husband is responsible to Christ, and Christ is responsible to God." God has made it clear that we are responsible for the spiritual climate in our home as well as for the climate of love and direction.

This is not to be interpreted as a cop-out on the part of your wife, for she still has the free will to choose whether she will trust Jesus Christ with her life. It is, though, a command for us as men to center our family life around the love of God. We are to take the initiative in prayer, in Bible reading and study, in thanking God for his provisions, in teaching our children spiritual truths from his Word. We are responsible for creating a climate in which Christ himself would feel welcome. Such a climate makes marriages and families joyful.

These, then, are God's two qualifying clauses when he commands you to take charge in your household:

First, *submit to one another*—giving her freedom to be herself, to contribute fully in the decision-making process. Being liberated enough to admit when you are wrong, without letting it threaten your sense of masculinity.

Then, *love her*—so wholeheartedly that she'll rarely doubt your love or resent your leadership. Firmness, tempered with gentleness. Christlike love.

Who's in charge at your house?

A big part of your wife's sense of security is your strong, consistent leadership in the home. Be a take-charge man. Lead her, with love.

13 Speaking the Truth in Love

To think justly, we must understand what others mean: to know the value of our thoughts, we must try their effect on other minds.
WILLIAM HAZLITT

I'm starting at my desk a little late tonight, but I don't mind at all. Kathy and I just spent two luxurious hours sitting on the sofa, discussing the pros and cons of her joining the sales force of a certain line of products. Financially, we knew, such employment would be advantageous. But is it something she would really enjoy doing?

This is where the conversation became fun, as well as revealing. As we moved past the facts and figures, we started to get down to our basic goals: "What's most important to us in life? What talents has God given us to nurture? What do we want to accomplish together?"

Our discussion has given both of us a deep sense of satisfaction. We've expressed what's on our minds, openly and freely. Put ourselves in the other person's shoes for a few moments. Shared ideas, visions, and dreams.

And we're closer now, because our time together has made us of "one mind" on several crucial issues.

It's a great feeling.

151

And it makes me wonder why good communication is often so hard for us husbands. Why do a majority of wives rate us consistently low in this area, when the importance of honest communication is so obvious?

"Tom and I don't talk nearly enough," one wife told me. "Sometimes I feel like we have a big guessing game going on in our marriage. I need for him to take the lead in communication, because whenever *I* do it I come off like the nagging wife."

"Why do you need communication?" I asked.

"Well, to avoid misunderstandings, and to clear up those that have already happened," she replied. "I guess most of all, just to know he loves me enough to listen and open up with me. But he usually seems preoccupied."

Are you like Tom? I know I tend to be. While our wives are begging for that good, loving conversation, we often find silence more comforting. Why? Well, let's be honest with ourselves:

Communication takes effort ... and we've had an exhausting day. We'd rather mull over the day in our minds than bring up anything fresh to discuss. Talking is hard work. Listening, even harder. Aren't we entitled to some laziness?

Amazingly, good communication has a way of rejuvenating a man. With the sharing of ideas and unloading of the mind comes a refreshing burst of energy. Happiness causes it. The interaction relieves tensions by confirming that all's OK on the home front, that the partnership is *working. We* need communication just as much as our wives do.

We allow too many distractions ... to steal our attention from her and the children. Unintentionally, sure. But how many times have I secretly wished Kathy wouldn't ask me a question during the evening newscast? Television (there's that culprit again), the newspaper, a book, a task to be done, and even other people can deplete my time and desire to interact with her.

We don't want to upset the apple cart ... and start an argument. Oh, please, not tonight.

A marriage counselor friend once told me of a couple that

came to him for counseling. "We've never had an argument in our lives," the husband announced proudly.

"How," asked my friend, "have you accomplished that?"

"We just don't talk," the wife replied.

In trying to avoid friction, their marital silent treatment had brought them to the brink of divorce. I've personally observed marriages just like theirs, in which the husband subscribed to the philosophy that "the less we talk, the less friction there'll be. So I'd better not bring this up..." For a while, there would be no *visible* friction, but inside both spouses the tension would build. Then, suddenly, POW! One minor incident would detonate a wild shouting match—all because things weren't discussed as they occurred. Their silence only turned them into human time bombs.

And I've seen other husbands who somehow manage to contain everything. Their tension never explodes, but just ticks away inside them throughout life as they continue to avoid disagreement. It doesn't take long for their health, nerves, and sexual performance to fail because of all that stored-up friction and resentment.

A primary principle of good communication is to *never fear disagreement.* In the next chapter, "How to Fight Like a Christian," we'll focus on this important area.

We have a subconscious fear of being vulnerable ... What if she spots a weakness in me, or an area I'm not really too sure about? Even worse, what if she's right and I'm wrong?

This pseudo-masculine trauma is so subtle, yet very much a part of our rationale for silence. We mimic the "strong, silent type" of male whose cool passivity denotes supreme confidence. But underneath is that nagging little fear: Do I really have anything worth saying? Do I want to expose the real me?

Such hesitation has no place in the genuine love relationship, for love encompasses an all-out, two-way trust. If I love Kathy and she loves me, I must trust her with my ideas— flimsy as some of them may be. I must trust that she will not reject or ridicule me because of my obvious weaknesses or inconsistencies. And she can expect the same acceptance from me.

When Adam and Eve were enjoying Eden, before they first disobeyed God, they were "naked, and were not ashamed." This obviously refers to a physical nakedness, but let's consider it in a total perspective for a moment. "Naked" implies a complete stripping away of facade and false pretenses. Adam and Eve, in their sinless state, trusted one another completely with their personhood. Nothing was held back for fear of rejection. And they "were not ashamed" of what they revealed to one another, for their love was solidified by intimate trust.

Do our wives know the real men inside their husbands? We have nothing to fear, men, in taking the initiative to reveal ourselves in our conversation. Total honesty—being "naked, and not ashamed"—can only deepen the quality of love between us and our loved ones.

What Is Good Communication?

The opposite of silence—merely talking—is not necessarily good communication. There are probably as many perpetual talkers in divorce courts today as there are silent couples. Good communication takes place when three important criteria are met:

1. *"Weak minds talk about people; mediocre minds talk about events; but great minds talk about ideas."* Why are people and the weather so easy to talk about? Because they don't require much thought or effort. People and events make good topics for discussion, but limiting communication strictly to them can turn families into boring gossips. Use people and events as springboards to more significant subjects.

Discussing *ideas* is what makes people grow into effective

thinkers and conversationalists. Ideas cause us to transcend everyday pettiness and rise to a higher plane of thoughts and dreams, and surprisingly, cause us to develop our skills of rationality while supporting those thoughts. Ideas draw people closer together as they ask, then answer, "What do you think about ...?" or "Why?" or "What if ...?"

2. *"The art of conversation is the art of hearing as well as of being heard."* (William Hazlitt) How easy it is to expound on our grandiose knowledge and opinions, but to listen with only half of one ear as the other person speaks! Ambrose Bierce has provided a perceptive, tongue-in-cheek definition of conversation as too many of us experience it:

> *Conversation, n. A fair for the display of the minor mental commodities, each exhibitor being too intent upon the arrangement of his own wares to observe those of his neighbor.*

The art of listening is an essential but oft-overlooked element of good communication. To listen effectively means focusing on the verbal and physical expressions of the speaker, hearing his complete message, and assimilating the message so that your mind holds a clear outline of the speaker's intent. If the outline is incomplete, the good listener will ask questions to clarify.

Recently, some communication experts have coined a term appropriate for our poor listening habits: "egospeak." The word means just what it says, that people simply enjoy listening to themselves more than to anyone else. Egospeak is thinking of what you're going to say next while another person is trying to talk to you. Jumping in before, or on, the other person's last word. Constantly trying to top the other person's story.

Watch carefully—you'll spot egospeak in almost every conversation these days. Genuine listening has become one of the endangered species. God gave each of us two ears and one mouth—perhaps he intended that we use them proportionally.

3. *"Speak the truth in love."* This biblical imperative distills all the elements of good communication into five powerful words:

"Speak" ...

and don't remain silent. Don't harbor ill feelings to the point of consuming resentment or anger.

"the truth" ...

as *observation,* not accusation. Get beyond the small talk to the things that really matter in your relationship.

"in love" ...

with a gentle tone of voice, at the right time and place. Be honest, yet sensitive to her feelings. Seek to bring out the best in her.

Getting Started

The key to initiating good communication at your house is simple: Ask questions:

With just a little practice, you'll soon learn which types of questions lead to the most fascinating types of conversation. "How are you feeling?" inevitably evokes either a "Fine" or a depressing organ recital. "Do you have choir practice tonight?" encourages only a "Yes" or a "No."

The principle of asking good questions is to ask *thought questions* which require more than a yes-or-no answer. These will ask a person how he feels *about* a topic, event, philosophy, etc., or perhaps stimulate him to brainstorm with you on topics for which he hasn't yet formed an opinion.

In the following pages, we've listed a number of questions that *every* husband and wife should frequently discuss together. Some of the subjects may scare you a bit—perhaps it's been years since you've communicated with her so deeply—but don't let them. With just a few suggestions for getting the most from your conversation time, you'll both be amazed at how much closer you feel as a result of talking together.

Those suggestions:

1. Don't force it. There will be many times when neither of you feel like discussing anything too deep. Let it happen naturally—sitting together on the couch, taking a walk, etc.

2. Listen. Look at her as she speaks, and as you speak to her. Respond with interest to what she has to say.

3. Never condemn an opinion by saying "That's stupid," or "It'll never work." That's the quickest way to drown good communication. Acknowledge her opinion, and ask questions to help her clarify it. Then, if you differ with her, introduce your view by saying something like, "Let's look at it from another angle, too..."

4. At first you may find that some thought questions grind to a halt before they even get started, due to an "I don't know," or "I haven't thought about it enough to form an opinion." This is a great opportunity for you to encourage each other to be vulnerable in exploring ideas: "Let's think out loud about it together." It's a fun, creative process.

5. When talking together about any of the following discussion questions, pursue each subject thoroughly by asking:

What is our present situation?
Why?
How does it affect our marriage?
What can we do about it?
OK—now what's the first step?

Questions
Every Husband
Should Talk About
with His Wife

Our marriage

1. What are some of the most important things we've learned since we've been married?
2. How has marriage enriched your life? Mine?

3. Are there areas in which you feel I can be providing stronger, more consistent leadership?
4. Do you feel that I spend enough quality time with you and the children?
5. How can I be more sensitive to your needs as a woman?
6. Have you sensed areas in which we find it hard to communicate?
7. Do you feel that I'm open enough in expressing love to you and the children?
8. Next time we can get away, what would you like to do together?
9. What has happened to us in the past year to draw us closer together?
10. Have you sensed tension between us and our in-laws?
11. Do you feel that I accept you as you are—or do I pressure you to change?
12. Do you feel threatened when I disagree with you, or make a decision you don't like?
13. Do I give you a fair voice in decision-making?
14. How can we disagree on something without it turning into a big fight?
15. Do I encourage you to express yourself freely?
16. Are there habits or mannerisms in my life-style that bug you?
17. Is there anything in our past that I've done that has caused some resentment to build up in you?
18. Do you like the general direction in which our marriage is headed?
19. What should our priorities be for:
    our personal development?
    our relationship?
    our children?
    accomplishments?
    spending?
    material needs?
    vocational goals?

20. What would you like to see us accomplish together this next year? Five years? Before retirement? After retirement?
21. Am I patient enough with you?
22. Would you like to spend more, or less, time together with other married couples?
23. Are you being fulfilled as a person? What are some areas you want to develop? How can I help you?
24. Is there anything in our marriage which is contrary to scriptural teaching?
25. What are some of the barriers to our communication which we can start to remove?
26. How can we encourage each other more?

Our sex life

1. Are you content with the frequency and the quality of our sexual relationship?
2. Do you feel that I fulfill your sexual needs?
3. Do I tend to be selfish during sex?
4. Are there things I do during sexual foreplay that you do not enjoy?
5. Are there techniques you would like me to use to arouse you more?
6. What do you like most about our sex life?
7. Are you willing to explore new techniques to lend more excitement and variety to our sexual relationship?

Our money

1. Do you ever sense frustration or resentment at the limitations of our salary? How can we encourage each other to be more positive?
2. Are you content with the way we handle our finances?
3. Do we act as though we believe God will provide all we need?
4. Do you feel we discuss the budget together sufficiently? Do I give you an adequate voice in planning?

5. Are we planning wisely for our financial future?
6. What spending could we have done without in the last few months?
7. Do we have more money than we really need?
8. Are we giving enough back to God through a tithe or special giving for the needs of others? What church, organization, or needy individual could we help financially?
9. What should be our policy regarding the use of the checkbook and the credit cards?
10. What can we be doing to teach the children financial wisdom?

Our children

1. Do our children know how much we love each other?
2. Do they know how much we love them? Do we tell them, and show it by our everyday actions?
3. Do you feel that I spend enough time playing and talking with them?
4. What are some positive ways we can encourage them:
   to be unselfish?
   to be loving to others?
   to have a good self-image?
   to be responsible?
   to develop their skills?
   to love God?
5. Do we agree on our philosophy of discipline for the children?
6. What should our policy be regarding the children's use of the TV set?
7. What are the values each of our children should hold to when they leave our home someday?
8. What practical skills should we be teaching them that will equip them for living?
9. What activities could we be doing together to increase family harmony and love?

Our spiritual development

1. Are you content with my relationship with the Lord?
2. Are you content with yours?
3. What can I be doing, as the spiritual leader of our home, to encourage you, me, and the children to live in a Christlike way?
4. Can we identify some specific areas in which we need to trust God more?
5. How can we encourage each other to trust him in every-thing?
6. What did you read from the Word this morning? How can we apply it today?
7. What has God recently done for us that we can thank him for?
8. What activities can we do together to teach Christian principles to our children in a meaningful way?
9. If someone came up to us and said, "Tell me how I can know God personally," what would we tell him?
10. Is our church meeting our spiritual needs and giving good instruction from the Word? If not, shall we look for one that does, or, what can we do to help our church accomplish its job more effectively?

Our possessions

1. Do you feel that I am meeting my responsibilities in keeping up with house and car maintenance?
2. What repairs or improvements would you like to see made soon?
3. Do we tend to be too materialistic?
4. Are there things that we really do need soon? In what order of priority?
5. Do we get angry if someone accidentally breaks a dish, or a piece of furniture, etc.?
6. Is our present dwelling too big or too small for us?
7. Does it have a happy atmosphere?
8. Is our present car too big or too small for us?

9. Do our clothes and the way we dress glorify God in their style and neatness?
10. What are ways in which we can maximize and make-do with the things we have?
11. Are we thankful for the things we have? Do we take good care of them?

Our protection

1. Is our insurance coverage adequate for:
   life
   medical and hospitalization
   unemployment
   car
   house
2. What would you do if you entered a room and found me lying on the floor unconscious? Or if I collapsed in a locked bathroom in the middle of the night?
3. What are some ways in which we can help fire-proof and burglar-proof our home?
4. Have we taught the children basic rules of bicycle and pedestrian safety? About strangers? Do they know their address and phone number? Do they know how to reach you or me in an emergency?
5. If you should ever be accosted by a strange man, do you know the most effective ways to dissuade him, using physical resistance if necessary?
6. What do we have to wake us in time in a nighttime fire? Do we all know what to do if a fire ever breaks out in our home? Or if an armed person breaks in?

General

1. What's the best thing that happened to you today?
2. What do you think of ... (a current event, etc.)?
3. How do you feel about ... (a current philosophy, etc.)?
4. *Why* do you feel this way?

5. What can we do for ... (someone in need, someone we love, etc.)?

As I was reading the paper this morning my eye caught a headline which read, "Annie Glenn Still in Orbit over John." The article tells how the marriage of U.S. Senator John Glenn, America's first astronaut to orbit the globe, is stronger than ever after thirty-one years. "We've always had this rule at our house," Annie Glenn tells the reporter. "No matter how hectic the schedule, we always had dinner together by candlelight. Maybe we ate hotdogs—but the ambience was there!

"We talked and listened to each other. I mean *really* listened. The communication has been paying off ever since."

As you seek to build such an intimacy with your own wife, I think you'll discover: Good communication in your marriage is well worth the effort.

14 How to Fight Like a Christian

*The aim of
argument, or of
discussion,
should not be
victory, but
progress.*
JOSEPH
JOUBERT

I'll never forget the hard knocks one of my best friends went through during the early months of his marriage. At least twice a month he'd drop by my office, looking as if he'd been up all night. "We almost got a divorce last night," he'd say, half in jest. But I could tell he and his wife had truly been through the wringer.

Since I was engaged to Kathy at that time, my friend's experiences made me wonder if I wanted to get married after all. I'd heard the saying that there are two sides to every argument—and they're usually married to each other. And the one about a husband who, when asked, "How's the wife?" replied, "I don't know. She's not speaking to me, and I'm in no mood to interrupt." Was I entering eternal bliss, or an eternal battleground?

A little of both, I later discovered. For no matter how strong our love for each other, Kathy and I do have our moments of battle. We don't exactly shine in those moments. We'd be fibbing if we said we enjoy them. But take two people:

> One male, one female,
> From totally different homes
> With different upbringings and experiences
> Each with emotional uniqueness
> With different likes and dislikes
> Each with some degree of independence
> And with some self-centeredness
> Living in the same house
> With different tasks and responsibilities
> Working from the same budget
> Trying to meet the same goals.

Will they agree on everything?

No way.

Despite their firm commitment of love and loyalty to one another, the fact that the husband and wife are two distinct people makes some degree of conflict inevitable. Disagreements and arguments *will* happen. Feelings will be stepped on and hurt. And there are even moments when their Camelot will be shattered by the thought, "Why did I ever marry you, anyway?"

It's all part of growing together.

The important thing is that we not sidestep the inevitable. To the couple committed to making their marriage work, "fighting" can be an excellent proving ground for their union. Of course, they don't seek conflict, but when it does occur they do not allow it to threaten their marital security. Through friction and argument, they can spot communication gaps and personal weaknesses, then resolve to encourage each other in solidifying those areas. But the key word is *can*.

Do you allow conflict to destroy the bond between you and your wife, or do you utilize conflict to help make your marriage better? It *can* serve as a strengthening agent— depending on how you decide to channel the disagreements when they happen.

Normally, you'll have three options. We might call the first one *the slow-cooker,* when for the sake of an artificial harmony you and/or your wife decide not to voice what's bothering you. But deep inside, the temperature rises: "How could she have said that about me after all I've done for her?" or "Again! That's the tenth time this month she's done that!" The tendency is to put the lid on it by clamming up, or to leave the room or house for a few hours until it all blows over. But it never really does. Instead, it blows up.

John B. Baren, assistant clinical professor of psychiatry at the University of California at Davis, agrees that silent battle will always do more harm than good: "When they [husband and wife] try to suppress anger, it usually comes out in other ways that can be harmful to the marriage. One of the typical ways it comes out is by putting each other down in front of others in a joking sense—when it isn't joking at all. It's related to unresolved anger—and unresolved anger can simmer inside a person for years and drive a wedge between the marriage partners."

Your second possible channel for disagreements is only slightly better than the first because it does involve verbalization. But it is verbalization on an almost pygmy level: *the boil-over*. After steeping in the slow-cooker, the problem erupts in a split second. One accusation after another is hurled, not out of desire for logic, but in a weak attempt at self-defense. Past offenses are dredged up and spat into the other's face. In-laws are brought into it. In other words, all the dirty tricks of arguing are flung about in an attempt to win the shouting match.

The boil-over can usually be attributed to selfishness on the part of each participant, for protection of the ego quickly takes precedence over the edifying of the marriage. Each line must top the other. Tempers sometimes get so heated that one spouse will fling a final zinger over his shoulder as he stomps out of the room. Then, it's the slow-cooker again. And neither the slow-cooker nor the boil-over have settled anything.

There must be a better way.

We'll call it *the peace table*. Here, conflicting viewpoints are aired in a context of presumed love and rationality, in which husband and wife attack *the problem* and not each other. At this discussion of disagreements, "speaking the truth in love" is the watchword. Each spouse is honest about his feelings, but phrases them in a way not intended to hurt the other.

Which of the three channels for disagreement do you and your wife normally utilize—the slow-cooker, the boil-over, or the peace table? Your answer will reveal whether you allow conflict to build your relationship, or weaken it.

To make conflict work *for* you, *try to turn every "fight" into a discussion.* This may require some "simmer down" time for both of you, so that you'll approach the peace table in more rational states of mind. But if you make it a family policy that the peace table will always follow a spat, even the most juvenile of arguments will be a learning experience from which your marriage can blossom.

For example, you find yourselves steeping in the slow-cooker. For the last several hours (or days), talk has been shallow and forced. You feel a degree of resentment toward your wife over something, or perhaps you sense her bitterness toward you.

As the leader in the home (and the one responsible for the climate of love and freedom there), *you* must take the initiative to break the tension by opening up the communication lines—even if she is the one who "started the whole thing." If the wife happens to be at fault, and she doesn't make the move to restore communication, it is deadly for the husband to refuse to take the initiative simply because his pride won't allow it.

In steering the situation from silence to discussion, avoid making blunt accusations, even if they are true. One young husband, in trying to apply these principles for the first time, couldn't figure out why his wife became only angrier when he suggested they talk it out.

"What did you say to her?" I asked him.

"Well," he said, "I remembered that honesty is important, so I said, 'Honey, you've been acting like a two-year-old. Come here and let's talk.' "

The young husband had missed another vital point of successful fighting, and that is to *try to make "I" statements instead of "you" statements*. "You" statements are accusatory and will only put your wife on the defensive, thus hindering further progress in communication. By saying "You've been acting like a two-year-old," this young husband brought conversation to a shuddering halt before it even began.

The "I" statement, however, helps pinpoint the problem without accusing anyone. If our friend had said, "Honey, I feel that something is wrong between us.... Please, let's sit down and talk about it," I can guarantee that his wife would have been much more receptive to the idea.

And if you and your wife find yourselves in a boil-over, the same principle applies: *Move yourselves from boil-over to discussion* by employing the "I" statement. Give the matter just enough time to cool down a bit, but don't leave it long enough for silent resentments to begin building. Again, you take the initiative (and there will be times, to be sure, when you just don't feel like it). "Honey," I might say after a boil-over with Kathy, "I feel bad about the way we just went about this problem. Our shouting didn't settle anything, and I was wrong for the way I exploded at you. Let's sit down and try it again—the right way."

It's natural for the egotistical male to want to say, "I was wrong—*and so were you*." Don't. She'll draw that conclusion herself after she sees how willing you are to make things right. Ogden Nash said it best when he wrote:

> To keep your marriage brimming
>   With love in the loving cup,
> When you're wrong, admit it,
>   When you're right, shut up.

The Pre-Fight Geneva Convention

We never *planned* a fight in our entire marriage—they all seem to develop naturally, like turbulent weather when warm and cold fronts meet.

So one of the best things Kathy and I did at the outset was to sit down and agree ahead of time on a set of fightin' rules. We didn't look forward to conflict, but we knew it was a sure thing. We wanted to be prepared. If it had to happen, we wanted to make sure it served to build our love rather than tear it down.

And someday, we realized, our own children would be watching us, learning how to settle their *own* differences from the way we settled ours.

If you and your wife have never agreed in advance on some guidelines for successful fighting, we heartily recommend them to help assure that you'll "speak the truth in love" when fighting time comes. Someday soon, sit down with your wife for your own Geneva Convention. To help you get started, we'd like to share our own rules with you.

When Trouble Is Brewing . . .

1. *We will recommit ourselves to making our marriage work.* Divorce isn't even an option. We're going to see this incident through, and build a better marriage because of it.
2. *We will attack the problem, not the person.* We will agree to disagree agreeably. Do the facts of this incident warrant the heated emotions we're showing? How about assuring each other, "Honey, I'm not sure I agree with you in this area, but I want you to know that I love you. Let's work this out as a team."
3. *We will always put people before things.* No broken dish, dented fender, damaged clothing, or scratched record album is just cause for lashing out at the other person.
4. *We will seek to give the benefit of the doubt to the other person.* Unless the other person admits otherwise, he meant well. He was trying as hard as he could to do the right thing.

5. *We will try to see the situation from the other's point of view*. Why *is* she so upset that I'm late and the roast is burned? How would I feel if *I* were in her shoes? Often the only difference between *marital* and *martial* is a misplaced "I."
6. *We will try to establish a degree of rationality ahead of time*. "We've got a problem here. Let's sit down and talk about it."
7. *Never in public*. Since we aren't auditioning for the soap operas, this disagreement is nobody's business but ours.
8. *We will try to use "I" statements instead of "you" statements*. We will make and discuss observations, not accusations:

"YOU" (ACCUSATION)
"You're insensitive!"
"Will you shut up and listen?"
"You never pay attention to me!"
"...and then you started yelling..."
"You broke my favorite vase!"

"I" (OBSERVATION)
"I feel misunderstood."
"I don't think we're communicating."
"I feel left out."
"It bothers me when we yell at each other."
"I'm upset that the vase is broken."

9. *We will watch our tone of voice*. Loudness and bitterness only indicate that we're losing control of ourselves.
10. *When an assertion is made about me, I'll try to repeat it verbatim before responding to it*. Besides helping to calm us both, this will verify that a) I've heard you correctly, and b) you said what you meant (and meant what you said).
11. *We will try not to be overly defensive, but open-minded to the possibility that we're wrong*. "Well, I may be wrong in this area. Let me tell you why I acted the way I did."

12. *We will avoid these statements: "You ALWAYS ..." and "You NEVER ..."* If these accusations are really true, they should have been brought up when they first occurred.

13. *We will not dredge up past sins of the other.* They should have been discussed and forgiven long ago. God "forgets" when he forgives; we should, too.

14. *No stomping out of the room.* This only prolongs the altercation and puts the problem back into the slow-cooker. Instead, let's stop for a breather by saying: "Honey, I need a few moments alone to calm down. I'm afraid I'll say something I don't really mean."

15. *We will talk it out to its conclusion.* Let's don't leave it hanging, only to build up inside us. Together, we'll explore: "What have we learned from all this? How was I wrong? What can we do to prevent this from happening again?"

16. *We will be sure to seek forgiveness and to forgive.* This is the most important part of the fight, for it determines whether we are merely lowering the heat under the cooker, or turning the fire off completely.

It takes two to tangle, and if I was a participant in the shouting match, I was part of the problem. Maybe she *was* misunderstanding me. Perhaps she *did* start it. Regardless, I joined right in by hollering back at her. And even if I was just one percent wrong and she 99 percent (which is not usually the case), I still need to ask forgiveness for my 1 percent.

The Magnetic
Power of
Forgiveness

Asking forgiveness is one of the most humbling, yet most gratifying acts you can perform for your marriage. Believe me, we know this from personal experience.

In one of our earliest fights, Kathy and I were both too

indignant to bother asking or granting forgiveness for each other. After our boil-over, we sat down and firmly made our points at the peace table, content that we had talked it all out. But I was still mad. So was she. We both fumed, silently, for several days afterward.

Then I read something that I really didn't want to see. Not at all. To back up my righteous indignation I was reading the Bible. And I came across these words: "... bearing with one another, and forgiving each other, whoever has a complaint against anyone; just as the Lord forgave you, so also should you" (Colossians 3:13).

Gulp.

Again, it came right down to the initiative a leader must take. If the Lord took that initiative to forgive me when I didn't even deserve it, then he intends for me to take the initiative to restore things with my wife. Regardless of whose fault it all was.

I had been blowing it by letting my pride say, "She's got to come to me first."

I wandered into the kitchen, where Kathy was fixing dinner. "Honey," I ventured, cautious of becoming vulnerable, "I've felt convicted about our fight the other day ... I don't think we finished it."

"What do you mean?" she said.

"Well, I was wrong for the way I shouted at you. I'm sorry—will you forgive me?"

Kathy smiled, put down some dishes, and melted into my arms. "I was just getting ready to ask you the same thing," she said. "Yes, I forgive you. Will you forgive me?"

"You bet," I said. From that moment on, we were committed to forgetting the hurts we'd been nursing for days. And it worked. The healing process took effect immediately and we were again happy together, talking and carrying on like nothing ever happened. We both remember the lesson of that fight, but the forgiveness was so complete that we can't even remember why we argued in the first place.

Remember: Time does *not* heal wounds—only forgiveness can do that. For without genuine forgiveness (verbalize it

173

and mean it!) time will simply give the hurt more opportunity to plant roots.

Never neglect the role of forgiveness in marital conflict. In spite of all the suggestions in this chapter for successful fighting, forgiveness is the one sure way to a happy outcome. With it comes an outflow of all the guilt, tension, and resentment that could have poisoned the relationship— because true forgiveness *forgets*.

No, fighting is never fun. But the liberated husband knows better than to allow the inevitable conflicts of marriage to pull him and his wife apart.

Together, agree ahead of time on a good set of "Rules to Fight By." Then, when conflict arises, talk about it! Take the lead in channeling the disagreement toward the peace table as soon as possible. *Listen* to each other, abiding by your rules. Discuss what you've learned from the experience. Apologize, and *forgive* each other.

So many couples today are missing out on the total healing that these steps can bring about—simply because they are afraid to "talk out" their conflicts. Their homes are filled with tension, awkward silence, steeping hatred, and bitterness.

Men, our homes needn't be that way. Make the effort to communicate openly, every day if possible. "Plug in" these principles for successful fighting at the first sight of trouble. If you do, you'll both begin to enjoy the delightful confidence that, in season and out of season, your marriage is going to make it.

Happy fighting!

15 Is Dad Really Necessary?

The work will wait while you show the child the rainbow, but the rainbow won't wait while you do the work.
PATRICIA CLAFFORD

If it weren't so tragic, I'd have to laugh.

Almost every day I read accounts in newspapers and magazines which describe a husband and wife something like this:

> Charles Durham, 46, serves as assistant to the vice-president of Acme Products, Inc., and is an avid golfer and hunter. His wife, Nancy, is the mother of three children.

Notice who is responsible for the children. Nancy, *the mother of*. No mention is made that Charles is *the father of*. Rather, he is removed from the home and placed on the corporate pedestal, briefcase in hand, to solve the problems of fiscal America.

"I earn the living; she raises the kids," he often boasts.

It's funny. Sad-funny. Somehow, Mom has been saddled with the responsibility of developing and disciplining young human lives. Dad has more important things to do: Sell the product. Earn the living. Win the world to a cause.

And society, with its modern success ethic, eggs him on. His frequent, prolonged absence from the house has become accepted as a natural part of "making it" in today's world.

One writer, David W. Augsburger, appropriately christens this phenomenon "the vanishing American father."

"He is wanted," Augsburger writes in *Cherishable: Love and Marriage,* "by his wife who would like to contact him for an appointment on their next anniversary. And by three children ages seven, nine and thirteen who would like to make his acquaintance...."

The vanishing American father. Are you one of them?

Is your primary role that of corporate assistant, printer, welder, accountant, preacher, office manager?

Or is it *husband and father?*

The way some of us have been working, one might wonder. And sadly, the person(s) wondering might be our own wives and children.

A group of 300 junior high boys were recently instructed to keep accurate records of how much time their fathers spent with them over a period of two weeks. Most boys reported that they saw their fathers only at the dinner table. Several never saw their father for days at a time—either he was traveling, or by the time he came home from work they were in bed. *The average time fathers spent alone with their sons in an entire week was seven and one-half minutes.*

A Virginia psychologist conducted a two-year study on children ages four to six, asking them the question, "Which do you like better: TV or Daddy?" As reported by United Press International, "44 percent of the children questioned chose television." Perhaps dads can rejoice that they landed 56 percent of the vote, but it's interesting to note that "only 20 percent of the children chose television when the choice was between their mothers or TV."

While society's work and success ethic has pulled Dad out of the home, psychologists, family counselors, and alert observers are pleading for him to return. As Augsburger writes:

> The most critical impact of father's disappearance is upon the children. A boy needs his father around to develop his images of what it means to be a man.... A daughter needs a father to develop her sense of femininity and to learn what to expect of masculinity.

Maybe you've seen some of the recent findings which link the father's absenteeism (and mother's resultant overbearance) to homosexual tendencies in children. Frightening, to say the least, when you learn that most homosexuals and lesbians are not born, but developed—quite often by the way their fathers relate (or fail to relate) to their wives and children.

In a piece titled "Fathers Wanted!" Paul Popenoe further confirms such findings:

> Research generally shows ... that perhaps the first five years of a boy's life are especially significant in respect to his development as a "normal" male. One study found that "father absence" in the lives of three-to-five year old children left them seriously handicapped; another study of four-to-eight year old children who for the first two years of their lives had been separated from their fathers, often due to the parent's military service, showed them perceived by their returned fathers to be "sissies."

Tragic results of the "vanishing father" go even further. When a young boy's home input is almost totally feminine, his interests are likely to be limited to feminine pursuits. He emulates Mom, because she is the primary example he sees. He may be confused when his peers play "man" games and copy "Dad" mannerisms. He might reach second grade before he learns how to use the toilet standing up. He may be inhibited by the opposite sex, and react by either withdrawing from or dominating young girls around him. And later in life, he may reject his parents completely because Dad didn't seem to love Mom, or care enough to be with his son.

Neither is the daughter of the often-gone father exempt from developmental risk. Studies by two researchers named Hetherington and Deur report that "Father-deprived girls showed extremes of either promiscuity or withdrawal from males."

Is Dad necessary?
You bet he is!

He is part of a God-designed *team,* and his teamwork is essential to the personal growth of his children. Asking Mom to do it all alone is like jumping off a careening two-person bobsled and expecting the brakeman to steer. *Unfair*—to her, and to the children. And to be honest, the father cheats himself out of a most rewarding challenge.

Dad is urgently needed! Together with Mom, he can help instill healthy perspectives on sexuality, love, discipline, roles, communication and caring. His kids won't accept a lecture-on-the-run. They couldn't care less about a disciplinary swat on the rear from a dad who hasn't been around much. *They will accept only his consistent personal example.*

I could cite dozens of heartbreaking stories of families destroyed by the neglect of well-intentioned fathers. Some of the dads are popular leaders in business, politics, and education. An alarming number of them are pastors and Christian leaders.

None of them intentionally forsook their duties of fatherhood, but the seeming importance of their jobs or ministries kept them late at the office or continually out of town. Some worked regular eight-to-five shifts, but on coming home in the evening were either too tired or too busy to play with their children. It wasn't that they didn't love their children—they *wished* they could spend more time ... especially when it became too late. What astonishment—what grief—when they learned that their teen-age son or daughter had run away from home, or shot heroin, or shacked up with someone of the opposite sex, or attempted suicide.

Perhaps these men's wives had accepted the fact that the job or ministry would keep their husbands away from home frequently. *But how many men asked their children?*

No job, no matter how noble, is worth shelving those precious people at home. As family counselor and author Howard Hendricks says, "It is a perverted altar" which sacrifices a man's relationship with wife and kids for the sake of the job or ministry.

"But I've got to work," says the frustrated father. "There's no way I can spend all the time at home that the wife does."

Yes, all of us must work—but that seven or eight-hour workday isn't considered "frequent, prolonged absence." You don't *need* all day with the child, and neither does Mom. That much doting would drive the kid crazy.

The vanishing father act happens in at least three ways. First, Dad may frequently work overtime into the evening hours and weekends. Or second, he may be in an itinerant profession, always speaking or caucusing in other cities around the country. Or third, he may only work a regular eight-hour day, but then is too tired, too busy, too complacent, or too "adult" to devote a generous parcel of undivided attention to the kids.

Now I don't know if you're one of those three types or not. Only you and God know that (and quite probably your wife and children). But would you take a few moments to muse on some very important questions? You see, I have a good feeling about you. I think you have the best of intentions for your kids. You *want* to be a successful father. But maybe—if you're like thousands of other contemporary dads—society has played a few tricks to pull your attention away from home.

After each of these questions, close your eyes for a moment and think through your own home situation. Take your time. Be honest with yourself.

1. *Do I really* know *my children?*

Think of each one by name and age. What are their ambitions? How are they different from each other? How do they differ from you? What are the growing pains they're experiencing? Do they feel free to share them with you—to ask questions?

2. *How do my children regard* me?

Are you just the man who comes home sighing in the evening? The man who wields the spanking stick? What do they know about you as a person? What do they know about your work, and why it's important to you and to them? Do they think of you as excess baggage, or as an authoritarian, or as the loving leader of the home? Do they respect that leadership?

3. *What attitudes or actions of mine have caused them to regard me in this way?*

Are you frequently too busy or out-of-town? Are "not now" and "don't bother me when I'm reading" a part of your vocabulary? Do you seem to spend more time disciplining them than you do talking or playing with them? Do you *talk* about living a balanced life, but in fact live quite out-of-balance?

4. *How do my children know that I love them?*

First of all, *do they know it?* Is it enough just to tell them? Do you find yourself buying things or giving money to show your love? Is that really effective? When you're home, is it a time of joy for them, or a time to tread softly?

5. *With the limited time that a father has, what should I be doing to best contribute to my child's development?*

What are the best things you can do for/with them to help develop them into balanced, total persons? (Think about this one on your own for awhile, then read on.)

I won't pretend for an instant to cover everything a parent needs to know about child-rearing. Whole libraries have been written on the subject, but unfortunately almost all the reading of such books has been done by mothers. Dads have a lot of catching up to do, and the best place to start would be the local Christian bookstore. Several recent titles are excellent for helping Mom and Dad synchronize their parental teamwork.

Instead of presenting an exhaustive treatise on effective

fatherhood, I'm going to write just a few of the basics straight from the heart. To me, these are the nonoptionals of fathering a child, gleaned from close observations of several smart dads I know. I'm convinced that these are The Three Most Important Things a Man Can Do for His Child.

ONE
Love
Your Wife

Unashamedly. Unreservedly. If you haven't guessed it by now, loving your wife is what most of this book is about.

A father returned home from work to hear his small son and daughter screaming at each other. Fearing that they were about to exchange blows, he asked, "What's going on here? What's wrong?"

The frowns turned to smiles. The little boy tilted his chin and said, "Nothing. We're just playing Mommy and Daddy."

A giant chunk of their ideas on how to treat the opposite sex will come just from watching you and your wife in everyday situations. Demean each other, and they will see no reason to respect you or anyone else. Romance each other, and they'll get the message: Love is good. Kindness is fun. Members of the opposite sex are to be respected.

Howard Hendricks firmly believes this principle. "The best thing a father can do for his son is to love his son's mother," he states in his family living seminars. "And the best thing a mother can do for her daughter is to love her daughter's father."

Dr. Henry Brandt, psychologist and lecturer, agrees. "Pay attention to the kind of person you are and to your relationship as partners," Brandt says, "and then do what comes naturally. I don't think you will need to worry about your children."

I'll never forget the "Family Hugs" that often took place in our kitchen as I was growing up. Toddling through the doorway, I'd see Dad wrapping Mom in his arms (not an unusual sight in our house). That made me feel good inside. So good that I couldn't resist joining them (after all, they had their private moments too). So I'd charge across the kitchen linoleum and wrap my arms around their legs. Mom and Dad were always happy to include me. If any other brothers were around, they would sometimes join in as the family circle got bigger and bigger.

Mom and Dad made our house a loving home, more by example than by lecture. We were secure as children because Dad took the lead in making the home atmosphere one of love and joy.

As John M. Drescher writes in *Eternity* magazine, "When a child knows parents love each other there is a security, stability and sacredness about life which is gained in no other way."

A close friend of mine, high on my list of smart husbands and fathers, told me this story the other day. A few nights before, his five-year-old son had awakened terrified from a nightmare. To comfort him, my friend's wife traded beds with the child, letting him sleep with Dad for the remainder of the night.

When daylight came, the boy began feeling sorry that he had caused such a hassle in the night. As his mother was waking up in his bed, he slipped back into his bedroom and gave her a big hug. "Thank you for taking care of me, Mom," he said. "I'm sorry I made you get up last night." Then, asking what he could do for her, he began waiting on Mom. He brought her some juice from the kitchen. Helped her tidy up the rooms. A keen observer of his father, the child wanted to show appreciation and love "just like Dad would do."

Children learn by watching and imitating. Whether you realize it or not, you are on constant display in your house. With young children around, you're about to be emulated at any moment.

So make your love for your wife *visible* to your children. Let them hold no doubt that she is "Number One" in your book of favorite people.

TWO
Develop
Your Child

Some parents operate under the assumption that all children have the devil in 'em—and that their job, as parents, is to beat the devil out through their children's britches. Discipline is a popular subject, and as you'll soon see I'm not about to ignore it. But often, as parents seek to drive the bad from a child, they forget how vital it is to point out the *good* in him.

A few weeks ago I heard a radio report which described a study of parents' comments to their children. It was found that the parents surveyed averaged ten negative comments for every one positive comment.

In Orlando, Florida, a three-year study of teachers revealed that 75 percent of teacher responses to children were negative. Yet, some experts in child psychology tell us that it takes four positive remarks to offset the damage to self-esteem caused by one negative comment!

"We live by encouragement and die without it—slowly, sadly and angrily," Celeste Holm, the popular theatrical actress, has said.

Dr. James Dobson, author of several excellent books on raising children, enforces the need for parental encouragement of the child:

> A child can learn to doubt his worth at home even when he is deeply loved by his parents! Destructive ideas find their way into his thinking process, leading him to conclude that he is ugly or incredibly stupid or that he has already proved himself to be a hopeless failure in life.

But encouragement, important as it is, is just one aspect of loving development. Your goals should include:
1. To help the child *know* he is loved.
2. To give the child a sense of security and acceptance.

183

3. To give the child a sense of self-worth.

4. To lead the child to healthy independence.

"Train up a child in the way he should go," Solomon writes in Proverbs 22:6, "and when he is old he will not depart from it."

"Fathers," Paul writes to the Christians in Ephesus, "do not provoke your children to anger, but bring them up in the discipline and instruction of the Lord" (Ephesians 6:4).

The balance is crucial. Discipline without development leads to anger and resentment. Development without discipline leads to chaos and rejection of authority. Blend the two together in an atmosphere of love, and your child will grow up to become the balanced person you want him to be.

What are some positive ways to develop your child?

1. *Listen to him.* Show a real interest in what he's doing and thinking. This means *total attention*—take your finger out of the newspaper, turn off the TV set, and sit down face to face with him.

If your child is young, get down on his level—literally! Can you imagine going through eight or nine years of life talking to people's kneecaps? You'll find communication more fun (for him and for you) if you can look each other in the eye.

Let him know that Dad is available and interested. A continued good rapport, started early, may cause both of you to someday ask, *"What* generation gap?"

2. *Accept him as a person.* Acceptance does *not* mean tolerating wrong. The spirit of approval means that you love your child even when he resists you or is in an ugly mood. He must know that his personal worth is not based on beauty, brains, or behavior, but on the simple fact that he is a person created by God.

Respect his uniqueness as a growing person. Question: Would you treat your best friends the way you treat your kids? ("Harriet, get your elbows off the table! George, quit slurping your milk!") Since your child should be among your best friends, learn to phrase your remarks to him as you would to a peer. This will help turn "nagging" into "instruction."

3. *Praise him.* Your child lives in a world of negatives. Most things he'd like to sample are still forbidden. The news is dismal. His teachers (and perhaps his parents) find negative criticism much easier to verbalize than the positive kind.

Look for the good in your child, and be quick to compliment him. Compliment his achievements, but don't hold achievements out as your standard of acceptance of him. Praise the fact that he tried and did his best. Reinforce him when he dresses well or grooms neatly. Be enthusiastic when he shares something with the family.

When I was a child, my folks used to rave with praise when I'd bring a picture that I'd "colored myself" home from school. It didn't matter that the giraffe was red, or that the cat had seven legs, or that the tree looked more like a Roto-Rooter truck. They liked it because it was from *me,* and I had exercised my creativity to its fledgling limit.

One of the biggest blunders a parent can commit is to let a moment for praise pass by in silence!

4. *Spend quality time with him.* This is probably the best way a dad can show his child that he loves him. The investment of time. *Never* attempt to substitute money-spending or "things" for time—in a child's book, the two just don't match up.

Some dads I know have initiated a family night at home, with notable success. One night a week is set aside for games, family crafts, charades, popcorn, etc. (not TV!)—wrapped up at the end with some innovative reading from a favorite book. Family night works best, they've found, when it is inviolable: No dinner invitation, business meeting, or social function is allowed to replace that evening with the kids.

My oldest brother Dale, a busy physician, enjoys the "Date with Dad" idea. Each of his three kids often has an exclusive "date night" for which the child can choose the activity. So far the Date with Dad has included hot dogs, ice cream cones, a movie, miniature golf, and even riding the car through an automatic car wash. It gives Dale opportunity to get to know each of his children as the unique individuals they are.

But special nights needn't be set aside in order to have quality time. What about that half hour before dinner after you get home from work? Your wife could use a break from overseeing the kids, and the evening paper can wait until later. Learn to use even the brief snatches of time available: "Hey, pal, we've got twenty minutes—why don't we give that basketball hoop a workout?" Whether you have just twenty minutes or three hours, he'll be honored that you want to spend that time with him.

In John M. Drescher's article in *Eternity* magazine he relates a beautiful story told by Arthur Gordon:

> "When I was around thirteen and my brother was ten," Gordon recalls, "father had promised to take us to the circus. But at lunch there was a phone call: Some urgent business required his attention downtown. My brother and I braced ourselves for the disappointment. Then we heard him say, 'No, I won't be down. It will have to wait.'
>
> "When he came back to the table, Mother smiled. 'The circus keeps coming back, you know.'
>
> " 'I know,' said Father. 'But childhood doesn't.' "

Want to make a good investment for your old age? Invest *time* with your child. Do the things *he* enjoys doing. Wholeheartedly.

5. *Give him meaningful responsibility.* Let the size of the task increase with the emotional maturity of the child. When the parent grants "important" responsibilities to the developing child and is faithful in thanking and appreciating him, the child's sense of "belonging" is secure.

Every child should have his own personal chores—picking up after himself, making and changing his bed, etc. As he gets older, some of the myriad household jobs should be parceled out to him (and to Dad, too). He'll have a better perspective of what it takes to keep a house going, but most important is the "community spirit" your family will find as you all pitch in together.

6. *Instruct him.* School is always in session when your child is growing up (but don't tell *him* that). Be alert for all the natural opportunities to teach values and practical skills.

Nature hikes are ideal for discussing creation and instilling a respect for God. A paper route or baby-sitting job is an excellent springboard for encouraging financial prudence.

Their most important training, however, is going to come from watching *you.* How do you and Mom iron out your disagreements? What do you say about your boss behind his back? Are you honest and fair in your dealings with others? Is a game played for fun, or is "winning" so important that any means of winning is justified?

The tactful dad can instruct his child without the child fully realizing it. Those times of talking and listening together. Playing together. Working on the car, or on a household project.

But there are also some times, unpleasant as they may seem, when instruction must occur at point-blank range...

THREE
Discipline
Your Child

The purpose of discipline is not to vent your wrath, but to correct and instruct the child. Have you ever met a child who enjoys being disciplined? I doubt it. Yet, that verse in Ephesians tells us, *"Fathers, don't provoke your children to anger ..."* Does this mean we should spare the rod?

No. That verse is addressed especially to fathers because Dad has more of a tendency to "provoke anger" in his kids. He might do it in one of three dangerous ways.

First, and what we see taking place in society today, is *underdisciplining.* If you asked your child, he'd probably inform you that he wouldn't mind underdiscipline a bit. But subconsciously, he knows that he needs it. A lack of consistent discipline will only frustrate him.

A friend of mine recently asked a grandmother, "Well, did you spoil your grandkids when you visited them over the weekend?"

The wise grandmother's reply: "Oh, you don't spoil a child by giving him *love*. You spoil him by *withholding discipline*."

Proverbs 19:18 tells us, "Discipline your son in his early years while there is hope. If you don't you will ruin his life" (TLB).

Underdiscipline might occur in these ways:

Giving in to the demands of the child. (Been watching at the supermarket checkout stands lately?)

Threatening the child but never following through with the discipline.

Threatening three or four times before administering disciplinary action. (One warning should be the limit.)

Inconsistency. Punishing after one occurrence; ignoring it after the next.

Mom and Dad disagreeing on whether to discipline. Protection and/or interference by grandparents.

Hollering at the child. (Fastest way to let him know he's gained control over you.)

Not suiting the discipline to the offense. (Swearing at Mom deserves more than a "Watch your language, Son.")

The second way we "provoke anger" is in *overdisciplining*. A happy home should have rules, but as few as possible. The Bible says that "His [God's] commandments are not burdensome" (1 John 5:3). So why should ours be?

Popular methods of overdiscipline include:

Punishing the child for doing something that's merely *in-*

convenient to the parent (instead of something that's really wrong).

Disciplining him in anger instead of love.

Punishing him for an *accident*. (Everyone spills his milk—usually Dad, right after he's spanked his child for doing the same thing.)

Saying "no" to everything without explaining the reasoning behind the answer.

Constantly criticizing the child.

Consider the observations of Dr. Haim Ginott:

> If a child lives with criticism, he does not learn responsibility; he learns to condemn and find fault in others. He learns to doubt his own judgment, to disparage his own ability and to distrust the intentions of others. Above all, he learns to live with continual expectation of impending doom.

The third way in which dads tend to provoke anger in their children is by *disciplining when they don't really have a right to.*

"Don't have a right to?" I hear some fathers saying. "What do you mean—he's *my* kid!"

Of course he's yours. But here's what I'm getting at: If you haven't first developed a *love relationship* with that child, you won't accomplish a thing by trying to discipline him!

Zealous parents will often come home from a family life seminar all "psyched" for applying the discipline. They've let their children get away with murder for fourteen or fifteen years, but no longer. Discipline time!

But all those strategies they learned at the seminar have little effect—in fact, the son or daughter seems more rebellious than ever.

What's needed? More rules?

No. More *time* from you. You must first inspire that long-overdue respect in your child by building the love relation-

189

ship you've let slide all these years. What does your son enjoy doing? Develop an interest in it so you can talk intelligently about it. Get out and do things together.

A parent only has the right to discipline his child if he also plays with his child. Why? Because discipline, to be effective, must be administered in the context of *love,* not legalism.

When that love relationship is solid (in *his* view as well as yours), then:

Don't withhold disciplinary action when it's needed. A bellowing child, age one to twenty-one, should never doubt who's in charge at your house.

Always make it clear that you despise *the behavior,* not the child. Instruct the child *(before* administering discipline) *why* the behavior is wrong. Let him know that you are hurt because of that behavior.

Suit the punishment to the individual. The "helping rod" is excellent for the young offender, but attempting to spank a seventeen-year-old will provoke anger. The aim is to teach, not humiliate. Also, be aware of the different temperaments of your children. To the sensitive one, a firm scolding may do the job of three spankings. To the strong-willed, however, three spankings may not be enough.

Then, always follow up the disciplinary action with love and instruction. With a younger child, this includes hugs and assurances that you love him. With an older one, a discussion of *why* the discipline was necessary. In either case, this is the time to assure him that the action was taken because you care about him. Seek to agree together that the offense was indeed wrong, and how it might be avoided in the future.

Parenthood was never meant to be easy. Someone once said that "It is ... sometimes easier to head an institute for the study of child guidance than it is to turn one brat into a decent human being." But when one realizes the magnitude—and the importance—of the task, it's evident that more and better leadership is needed by dads all across the country.

Dad *is* necessary. If there are children in your house, *you're urgently needed there!*

Shakespeare wrote, "It is a wise father who knows his child." As you invest that quality time and attention your children so desperately need of you, I have no doubt that you'll also find ... it's a *happy* father who knows his child.

16
Until Debt Do Us Part

In disgust, Phil threw the checkbook into the desk drawer. "Well, that shoots it for this month," he sighed. "No nights out for us."

"How bad is it, Dear?" Bev asked.

"Well, we made it through our mortgage payment, insurance, and utilities. And we can pay the orthodontist *if* you can get by on five dollars less each week for groceries."

"Ugh," Bev said.

"And Master Charge and BankAmericard will just have to wait...."

"What about Sears?"

"*And* Sears ..."

"What about our stereo payments?"

"*And* Blake's Stereo Supply ..."

"And our new dining table?"

"*And* Main Street Furniture ..."

There was a pause, the kind that both Phil and Bev had learned to dread. In their marriage, it usually signaled the calm before the storm.

"Phil—"

"Please don't say it, Bev. We've been through all this be-fore..."

"I *know* we have, Phil, but I hate being this far in debt."

"I don't want to hear it again."

"But you *know* we shouldn't have taken that three-day trip on BankAmericard last month. I *knew* we were spend-ing too much."

"You didn't seem to think so at the time ..."

"Oh, so it's all my fault, right?"

"No, Bev, it's not all your fault. I just felt that we really needed that trip together, that's all."

"Sure, like we need another bill or two ..."

"OK, OK. Will you quit complaining?"

"I'm just sick of not having any money, that's all. Every month it's been this way, and if we ever *do* get some extra, we blow it."

The atmosphere in Phil and Bev's living room grew icy silent. *Why don't we ever have enough money?* Bev was fuming. *Jack and Lorraine never seem to have our problem. Why can't we get nice clothes and furniture and still go out evenings like they do?*

I don't like it any better than she does, Phil scowled. *I just wish she wouldn't gripe, gripe, gripe. Who does she think I am, the Shah of Iran? I do the best I can. But how are we ever going to get out of this mess?*

Money problems.

For those of us in the million-dollar-a-year-and-under bracket, they're almost as inevitable as the national debt. And sometimes they may seem to loom as large.

Money worries can set even the most intimate marriages on edge. Blissful young couples tell me, "Money doesn't matter—our love is greater than that." I heartily commend their love, but with the same breath I must add: Money *does* matter. Don't let it become your main focus in life, but don't deny its worth, either. The "money will take care of itself" attitude is one of the most predictable ways to see red in the family budget, and to arouse feelings of insecurity (especially in her); anxiety (especially in him); defensiveness (in both); and even suspicion.

Which points up two cold, hard facts which every married man must grapple with. First, poor money management and marriage mix about as well as drinking with driving. Either way, you're on a collision course. And second, financial fiasco *is* a prevalent cause of damage in today's home.

One estimate has it that close to *one-half* of the nation's divorces are due to differences of opinion on how to handle the family finances. And those couples are comparatively lucky: A recent sociological study in Chicago found that some 40.2 percent of all *desertion* cases were rooted in monetary tension between the husband and wife—as were 45 percent of the reported cases of *cruelty*.

Even those couples committed to loving each other for life are not exempt from the money strain. The National Foundation for Consumer Credit estimates that five or six of every 100 American families are in serious financial trouble today. A while back I listened in shock as I heard some cash experts claim that the average American family operates just three weeks from bankruptcy. And a glance at the average household budget sheet might show us why a *Ladies Home Journal* survey revealed that 70 percent of all our worries these days are about money.

Where do all the troubles come from? Whether we're in deep trouble or merely seeking to avoid it in the future, identifying the major problem sources is half the battle. And there's no denying the existence of the Seven Money Monsters:

The Inflation Monster. He has leered at us all in recent years, to the point where the real disposable income of the American family has actually declined. Even with salary increases, the combination of inflation and increased taxes has slenderized our ability to purchase things or save money.

The Emergency Monster. This creature is always rude, though he visits us in forms both small and large. In his smaller moments he is the unexpected tax increase due and payable last week, the unexpected guests ("Hi! Thought we'd fly in for a couple of weeks"), the ring job on the car, and myriad others. In the Emergency Monster's more obese forms, he is the job layoff, the extended hospital stay, the emergency surgery, the fire or burglary. In the next chapter, we'll be discussing how to minimize the potency of the monsters Inflation and Emergency.

The "Thing" Monster. While inflation and emergencies cannot be helped, the "Thing" Monster and his four following cronies *can.* They are attitudes and misconceptions about money which we've allowed to infiltrate our thinking. "Thing" is the product of an otherwise sound free-enterprise system—his advertisements bombard us right and left until our desire for the new golf clubs, then the new car, then the new blender, then the new book, then the new calculator, then the new bowling ball becomes insatiable. As part of our misguided success ethic, our society has taken on a "thing" orientation which tends to emphasize the building of inventory over the building of character.

The "Image-Building" Monster. This is the wart-nosed brother to "Thing." He insists that the "Thing" match the position or occasion, or else we are square, uncool, unmanly, out-of-it. The executive must drive the shiny new Mark IV, fly first class, wear white belt and shoes. The tennis buff will improve his game 50 percent with the new Jimmy Connors tennis shorts and shirt (and matching headband, wristband, warmups, socks, and duffle bag). A job with a certain income requires the proper house, car, pool, and automatic garage door opener.

The "Keeping Up" Monster. This monster often appears cross-eyed from constantly watching others out of the corner of his eye. He's in close company with the "Thing" and the "Image-Builder." If Jones buys a new car, "Keeping Up" insists it's time we get one too. If Smith gets a promotion and travels to Europe on the extra salary, "Keeping Up" convinces us that we deserve a big vacation just as much as Smith—even if our salary still only allows for, say, a trip to McDonald's once a month. This particular money monster will even pit husband against wife: If wife gets new outfit, husband is then justified in buying new tool set. And vice versa.

The "Save! Save!" Monster. How often in each day do we hear "Save 20 Percent!" Save Five Dollars Off Regular Price!" "Come on Down and Buy Your New Sofa Now—and Save!!!" Save? Think about it. Despite this monster's lucrative deals, there is no way that one *saves* money when one *spends* it. He will only have fewer dollars in his pocket, or more added to his charge account, than before. We do not save by spending, no matter how much the price has been reduced. Hundreds of families every year "save" themselves straight to bankruptcy court by grabbing more bargains than they can pay for.

The "Easy Credit!" Monster. We'll usually find him drooling over the shoulder of the "Save! Save!" Monster— right there to "make that bargain purchase possible" when we've run out of cash. When properly used, credit can be a tremendous asset to a family's life, but recent figures show that for a growing number of couples, those loans and little pieces of plastic spell trouble. The U.S. Bureau of Labor and Statistics, in a survey of 10,813 families in 91 cities, discovered that the average family spends each year *$400 more than it earns.* Added to that amount would be the $225 in *service charges* the average American couple pays out each year. The "Easy Credit!" Monster has bedeviled a lot of well-intentioned people. His motto: "Buy now, think later."

The Seven Money Monsters are not all new to the twentieth century. Indeed, the Bible is filled with sound advice to the family provider and businessman. Proverbs alone presents more than forty references to integrity in money management. *Regarding credit:* "The rich rules over the poor, and the borrower becomes the lender's slave." *Regarding casual borrowing or co-signing of notes:* "Do not be among those who give pledges, among those who become sureties for debts. If you have nothing with which to pay, why should he take your bed from under you?" *And about making wealth your goal in life:* "Do not weary yourself to gain

197

wealth; cease from your consideration of it. When you set your eyes on it, it is gone. For wealth certainly makes itself wings, like an eagle that flies toward the heavens."

But while it is vanity to chase after wealth, God does not deny that money is a necessity for existence, for sharing with others, and for recreation and enjoyment. Among the important lessons in Christ's "Parable of the Talents" in Matthew 25 is the fact that God disapproves of slothfulness when it comes to financial matters, and that he uses money as a test of our faithfulness to him.

So if our own common sense doesn't make the point strongly enough, we have the command direct from God to exercise wisdom in all money matters. Have you ever stopped to think about how much money you have been entrusted with during life? Think of it this way: If you were twenty years old in 1970, and would earn an average income the rest of your lifetime, you would eventually earn and manage close to *three-quarters of a million dollars!*

For the average earners like Phil and Bev, then, *more money* is really not the answer. More money just has a way of generating more spending (and more debt). The answer to their need is not more money, but *better control* of what they do have.

Financial freedom.

Now financial freedom does not mean the freedom from responsibility, nor does it mean having so much money that you can spend "freely" on practically anything. It entails three objectives which should be at the heart of every couple's financial plan.

Financial Freedom Is . . .

To be free of financial bondage involves:

1. *Freedom from Financial Debt*—That is, the debt which goes far beyond the sensible limit for your own income level. We'll explore some good ways to avoid this pitfall. And in

case you're already in over your head, there *are* some alternatives to further borrowing.

2. *Freedom from Financial Worry*—As if debt weren't enough of a strain, there may be an increasing concern over the inability to "make ends meet" and even over possible financial doom. With some practical budgeting and planning ahead, anxiety can usually be erased from next month's budget.

3. *Freedom from Financial Selfishness*—Money is simply a tool to help us survive, enjoy life healthfully, and share with others in need. But ever since monetary values were invented, there has been the strong yearning to make more, have more, and spend more. The simple tool becomes an ultimate goal, blurring one's real purpose in life. As a result, that same money which is meant to make life pleasant spurs financial paranoia, misery, and even underhandedness. But we can be liberated from the fiscal treadmill by keeping in mind the principle of our "Tower of Success": *Success is what you are*—not what you do or how much you make.

How to Spot
Danger Ahead . . .

There are definite warning signs of impending disaster, says the National Foundation for Consumer Credit. If you answer "YES" to at least two of the first six questions below, you've got potential problems. If you answer "YES" to three or more, you're already in trouble.

YES NO

1. ___ ___ Do you charge small day-to-day expenditures such as groceries and toiletries because you don't have the money to pay for them?
2. ___ ___ Have you recently postponed paying a bill "until next month" due to lack of funds to cover it?

3. ___ ___ Do you have to borrow money to pay fixed expenses such as quarterly tax payments, insurance premiums, even low installments?

4. ___ ___ Do annual payments on long-term debts amount to more than 20 percent of your annual income?

5. ___ ___ Are you unable to say exactly how much money you owe on installment and other long-term debts?

6. ___ ___ Are you receiving some phone calls or letters from creditors demanding payment of overdue bills?

In addition to the above questions, most family financial counselors are in agreement on several other caution signals which would warrant a close look at one's financial situation. So let's take the test further:

YES NO

7. ___ ___ Have you been shuffling funds about, using cash you had originally set aside for other purposes?

8. ___ ___ Are you dipping into reserves (savings accounts, not-yet-matured bonds, etc.) to pay current bills?

9. ___ ___ Are you borrowing to pay for items you formerly bought with cash?

10. ___ ___ Do you have less than two months' take-home pay in a readily available savings account for emergencies?

11. ___ ___ Are you taking out a new loan to pay an old one, or extending an old loan in order to lower monthly payments?

12. ___ ___ Do your monthly installment debts (other than your home mortgage) exceed 20 percent of your monthly take-home pay?

13. ___ ___ Have you been consistently paying only the

minimum amount due each month on charge
accounts?

14. ____ ____ Do you find it necessary to rely on extra income to make ends meet?

15. ____ ____ Have you been repeatedly unsuccessful in
saving for near-future needs, such as a refrigerator, vacation, or car?

16. ____ ____ Have you been unable to save for the long-
term goals, such as retirement, college for the
children, etc?

17. ____ ____ Have you and your wife had frequent arguments based on money problems?

18. ____ ____ Have you often found yourself scheming
about get-rich-quick ideas?

19. ____ ____ Do you have a consuming desire to build your
bank account far beyond, say, a level comparable to six months' take-home pay?

20. ____ ____ Have you recently engaged in suspicious or
dishonest money dealings ... OR, have you
been seriously considering it?

21. ____ ____ Does your list of "things-I've-just-got-to-
have" keep on growing, no matter how many
of the items you buy?

22. ____ ____ Have you found yourself hesitant to tithe your
income, or to give to someone in need (without
expecting a returned favor)?

As you look back through your answers, you'll notice that
this little self-test deals with all three areas of financial
bondage: debt, worry, and selfishness. If you checked "YES"
on any question, you may find it helpful to analyze, then
write in the margin, which aspect of financial bondage that
particular question involves. (Some questions might entail
all three, for debt, worry, and selfishness are so closely related that one often spawns another.)

For example, let's say you marked "YES" on question
#12. This would definitely indicate debt, for most financial
counselors set a debt of 20 percent of your take-home pay as

the maximum workable limit. If you checked "YES," mark "DEBT" in the margin beside the question.

Then, if your degree of monthly debt is causing some *worries* for you or your family, write "WORRY" in the margin also. This exercise will help you see what type of financial bondage you *might* be headed for, as well as what you're doing to speed up the trip.

17 Five Safeguards of Your Financial Freedom

There was a time when a fool and his money were soon parted, but now it happens to everybody.
ADLAI STEVENSON

If your answers to the questions in our previous chapter were all or mostly "NO," then chances are your money situation is in good shape. But this does not mean you can ease up on the dollar discipline. In fact, a family can slip into financial bondage so quickly, and in such subtle ways, that wisdom and caution must become a way of life. One large untimely purchase, one bad investment, one emergency—sometimes that's all it takes to plummet a family budget from "adequate" to "tragic."

It's impossible to predict what *could* happen in your family's finances, but you need not live in fear of tragedy if you're doing all you can to prevent needless mistakes. By following five sensible safeguards, most couples will get through life just fine—with their needs met, a "plus" balance in their savings account, and sufficient extra for giving, recreation, and enjoyment.

SAFEGUARD 1
Talk About Money!

Financial differences, along with sexual maladjustment, is one of the biggest causes of disharmony in modern marriages. We'll discuss sexual communication in the next chapters. Here, we must address that other vital area of communication in which we husbands must take the initiative.

In the vignette that led off the last chapter, Phil and Bev were *not* really communicating about money. They had reached the boil-over stage. Their explosion was the result of the "slow-cooker" process, in which each failed to communicate while harboring doubts and disagreements on their budget practices. *Women's Day* magazine, in an article titled, "Why Some People Spend Too Much," sees problems like Phil and Bev's this way:

> One thing that characterizes almost all couples with money troubles is that they seldom discuss financial matters. They have such unrealistic ideas about money [that] the only way to hold onto their fantasies is to avoid talking about them.

And according to the author of this article, poor communication in *any* aspect of marriage (not just money matters) can lead to financial foolishness:

> Some husbands and wives punish each other by buying things they can't afford after an unresolved fight. The wife "shows him" by indulging in a new fur coat; he retaliates by buying the boat they had decided was beyond their means ... and so it goes.

The budget, just like everything else in a marriage, must be handled through intimate teamwork between the husband and wife. While one of you *administrates* the family finances, the other spouse should serve as full-time consultant. Again, it all boils down to the partnership of marriage—and when one partner makes a big-money decision without consulting the other, there can be chaos in the "company."

Many times I've heard husbands ask, "Who should handle the family budget?" Several years back, I would have answered, "Definitely the husband—it's part of his leadership responsibility."

Recently, however, I've had opportunity to observe how several couples manage their money, and I've had a growing conviction that the family budget administrator need not necessarily be the husband. Some husbands are out of town too much, or otherwise too busy, to do a proficient job of managing money (and other things) at home. Other husbands admit that their aptitude for budget-keeping is about as high as that of Congress. So I've concluded that the wise family leader does not insist on administering the budget simply because he is the leader. As we stated in "Who's in Charge?" an important part of wise leadership is knowing when to *delegate* a responsibility to the wife. If she's more prudent in money matters, chances are *she* ought to be handling the budget.

But the teamwork must still take place. If you haven't discussed the family's finances together recently, make a date with your wife for a good two-hour session together. Talk about your priorities for spending and saving. Pinpoint any areas where you have recently spent foolishly. Agree on some rules you'll both follow in order to better communicate about the family budget. Our chapter on "Speaking the Truth in Love" lists some money questions that may help you get started.

205

SAFEGUARD 2
Educate Yourself
About Money
Management.

I never took a civics course, so I've had to learn most everything the hard way. I learned about possible tax deductions while paying the taxes I could have legally avoided. I learned about credit by buying just a little too much (for my budget) on Master Charge. I learned to say "No" after I'd said "Yes" to too many "Money Monsters."

They say that one of the best ways to learn is from your mistakes, but sometimes I wish that I had begun to actually *study* the principles of money management sooner than I did. There are some excellent books in circulation on this subject, and you may find it worthwhile to invest in a few for your own enlightenment. Sylvia Porter's *Money Book* is a sound "Money Management 101" course. Other books deal more specifically with budgets, taxes, credit, investments, etc.

If you're able to swing a slightly larger investment, I'm told that the First National Bank of Boston offers a home study course in personal financial planning. The fee is a reasonable $36. For information, write to:

> First National Bank of Boston
> 100 Federal
> Boston, MA 02241

Whether from your mistakes and those made by others, or from books and courses, seek to educate yourselves about financial management. The best place to start might be the book of Proverbs. Then talk to qualified people, read and underline some books, and consider a course or two. It isn't as if you were seeking ways to become filthy rich; rather, you will be gaining knowledge to help you be better managers of what you already have.

SAFEGUARD 3
Avoid Heavy Debt
Like the Plague.

Credit can be a tremendous asset to a family who has learned to respect it for what it is: a tool to help them acquire certain *necessary* items that would otherwise be impossible. Without credit, most of us would be unable to own a house or property and many would have to forego the convenience of the automobile.

But, like most other "good things" in life, credit is meant to be used wisely and not abused. Every family budget has its debt limit. To go beyond that limit is to consign oneself to becoming "the lender's slave."

"Debt" is technically defined as having more total liabilities for money, goods, and services than total assets. In other words, the sum total of what you owe exceeds the sum total of what you own.

In setting up our own financial plan, Kathy and I weighed the technical definition of "debt" and decided that we wanted to play it even safer. We decided that for our purposes (except for a future house or a big emergency) we would try to never borrow more than we already held in *liquid assets* (cash readily available, such as in savings accounts). This has helped us in two ways: first, it motivates us to keep saving steadily; and second, it gives us a self-imposed "borrowing limit" which has helped us evaluate whether we really do need that thing for which we are tempted to borrow.

But that decision is only the foundation for *several* principles we've employed to help us avoid heavy debt. If you've found that you and your wife need to watch your spending more closely, perhaps these guidelines will be valuable to you, too:

Guard against the "Money Monsters." We can combat Inflation with smart budgeting and Emergency with wise planning, but heading off the brothers Thing, Image-Building, Keeping Up, "Save! Save!" and "Easy Credit!" re-

207

quires a daily dose of will power. As you watch TV, read the ads, or browse through the stores, don't let the Money Monsters trick you into thinking you need something you really don't.

Agree on a family priority list–and stick to it! Together, list all the items that are *needed*—the new jeans for Bobby, a home fire-detection system, new shoes for the wife, a new floor lamp, a vacuum cleaner that works, etc. Then go back and decide which is the most urgent. Place a "1" beside that item, then proceed to rate the remaining needs in the order of their importance. Then, unless your town comes up with an unbeatable sale on a lesser item, follow your priority list by saving for (or charging and paying off as soon as possible) *one item* at a time.

You can also make such a list for your *wants*—such as a dishwasher, set of golf clubs, extra-special vacation, etc. But it's important that you hold a regular family financial council to evaluate allocations to the "wants" and the "needs."

Use "list shopping" to resist the impulse items. This technique is especially important in the supermarket or variety store, where shrewd merchandisers strategically place their products to catch the eye. Those extra soft drinks, potato chips, cookies, nuts, gum, lifesavers, and magazines add up. Products placed at the checkout stand are actually called "impulse items" by the marketing brains, for the shopper rarely actually *plans* to get them—they just seem nice at the time. Steer clear by sticking to the essentials on your list.

Wait for the right sale or season. For awhile, it seemed inevitable. I'd purchase a new set of tires for the car at full price, only to see them go on sale at 40 percent off just two weeks later. Or I'd find a "special" for $10 off, three days before the same item was reduced to half price. The lesson: Keep alert for the sales that can save you money and heavy debt.

And if you're in the market for seasonal items, you'll find the best sales at the close of the season in which they would be used. Buy skis and winter clothes in the spring, and backpacks, air-conditioners, golf clubs, and summer clothes in the fall. Consider buying this year's model car in the fall just as the next year's models are moving in. And the weeks after Christmas are good ones for bargains in practically any department.

Try not to browse in stores with the checkbook or large sums of cash. While I'd like to think that my financial constitution has grown stronger, I still must recognize that I can be weak. Yes, I'd *love* to have that new tennis racket. But there's no way we can manage it this month, and it'd be smarter to wait until fall anyway.

But it's amazing how easy it is to talk yourself into something when you've got cash in hand (I've done it more than once). The culprit could be several "little things" that would be nice-but-not-necessary, and these can often be more deceptive than the major purchases. If you and your wife have discerned a weakness in this area, try to cut down on your browsing time in stores—especially when you have money in your pockets.

Easy credit? Watch it! Unless you can pay off your "charge" at the end of the same month, you are paying *extra* money for the privilege of charging it. On most credit cards, finance charges run 1½ percent per month, which doesn't sound too formidable until you multiply it by twelve months. That gives you the *annual percentage rate of 18 percent!* For a large purchase, you'll probably pay less interest by borrowing from your bank.

You and your wife will want to talk over the whole subject of credit and decide on your own guidelines to suit your income and life-style. Kathy and I, knowing how easily we could be swept up by a new TV set or a gizmo we don't really need, have agreed that we will first *leave the store* and try to discuss, pray, and "sleep on" a major purchase before committing ourselves to additional installment payments.

We've also held ourselves to the rule that we will carry our Master Charge or BankAmericard with us for emergency purposes, but we'll guard against indiscriminate charges (and a frayed marriage) by first discussing and agreeing *together* on any potential installment purchase that could not be paid off at the end of the same month.

If an item (or an accumulation of items) can be paid for at the end of the purchase month, then the buyer is merely "borrowing" at no interest and taking advantage of the credit card in lieu of cash. Even if his purchases are small enough to be paid for within two or three months, his cost of borrowing hasn't been too high. But when that new possession takes six months, a year, or longer to pay for, that 18 percent annual rate makes credit expensive.

A guideline which every couple should try to observe is their "Personal Debt Limit." As we've already seen, most financial advisors feel you're headed for trouble if you are spending more than 20 percent of your monthly take-home pay on debt repayment (not including home mortgage). If you're deeply in debt already, it's probably wisest to stay with a 20 percent debt elimination allotment until your obligations are met. But if you wish to steer clear of trouble after that (or in the first place), Sylvia Porter offers an easy formula for finding your personal debt limit:

> Do not owe more than 10 percent of the amount you could pay for out of your income within the next eighteen months.... say your take-home pay is $800 a month; that gives you 10 percent or $80 for debt repayments each month. With this monthly sum you could pay off $1,500 over eighteen months. Your safe debt limit would be about $1,500.

Find your personal debt ceiling and then stick to it. Don't put any new purchases on credit unless: 1) You can pay for them at the end of the purchase month *in addition to* your regular installment payment on that particular account, or 2) it does not shoot your total debts above your personal debt limit.

Try not to borrow heavily on depreciating or consumable items. There will be exceptions to this guideline, for the automobile is one of the fastest-depreciating commodities around and few people are able to pay cash for one. But in general, borrowing on depreciating or consumable items is just bad investment.

And depressing. Have you ever spent the long, cold winter paying for that two-week vacation you took the summer before? Or have you watched furniture, clothing, or sporting goods deteriorate before you have paid for them?

If possible, set up an additional savings account for your short-term needs so you'll be able to either pay in full or put down a substantial down payment. Don't be fooled by loud advertisers who proclaim: "No down payment!" or "Only ten dollars down!" These simply mean that your total debt will be larger, requiring *more* months of *heavier* installments. Take the time and effort to save enough so you can make the biggest down payment possible.

SAFEGUARD 4
Conquer Worry with
a Smart Budget.

The best way to avoid anxiety over finances is to spend some quality time *now* in preparation. That means setting down a realistic budget which meets not only your current needs but provides a cushion fund for the future.

Smart budgeters find four questions particularly helpful as they weigh the facts and figures. If you find yourself unsatisfied with your present budgeting system, I would suggest that you and your wife sit down with pencil and paper and ask yourselves:

What do we have coming in each month? Write down your monthly take-home pay from all wages, then add any other income you receive on a monthly basis. If you expect some lump income such as dividends or a Christmas bonus, divide these lump amounts by twelve to give you the monthly average.

What are our fixed expenses? "Fixed expenses," for our purposes, do *not* include installment payments on any household, personal, or luxury items—we'll get to those a bit later. Fixed expenses are those regular monthly expenditures that are virtually nonoptional for the circumstances in which you've chosen to live. Included are your rental or mortgage payments; house, car, life and health insurance; and local taxes. (You'll probably have some insurance premiums or taxes that are due quarterly, semi-annually or annually; divide these by twelve to determine your monthly average.)

Unfortunately, many couples listing their fixed expenses stop right there. They ignore two other important items, often relegating them to the see-if-we-have-anything-left-after-paying-the-bills pile.

Tithe and savings.

Both are essential to one's freedom from financial bondage.

The *tithe* helps insure freedom from financial selfishness. It is a regular gift to God's work or to people in need, usually a fixed percentage of one's monthly income.

Throughout the Bible, God promises us that he will shower his blessings on those believers who faithfully and lovingly contribute to his Kingdom. Proverbs 3:9, 10, for example, implores us to "Honor the Lord from your wealth, and from the first of all your produce; so your barns will be filled with plenty, and your vats will overflow with new wine."

But the impetus behind the tithe must not be *to receive;* rather, it is to be an offering of love for God and a desire to further spread his love and forgiveness around the world. The tithe can be given to your church, a Christian organization or mission work, or to individual staff of such works who must raise personal support. And though this shouldn't be your motivation, such gifts are almost all tax deductible.

If you haven't already, discover the joy of giving financially. Give the tithe in a spirit of happiness and prayer for those people or causes you're supporting. God makes no demands about specific amounts. Most Christians follow the example of a group in the Old Testament, who gave the first one-tenth of their produce to the Lord's work. Many people enjoy giving much more, realizing with calm assurance that God will be faithful in meeting their needs.

Savings run a close second to the tithe as the most-postponed (or forgotten) aspect of financial planning. A good savings strategy on your part will help insure freedom from financial worry and future debt.

"But we just aren't able to save anything these days," I've heard more than one couple plead. "Inflation just about wipes us out every month. And then whenever we do stash some funds away, they don't seem to stay there very long."

Common problems, I know. But in most cases, nothing that a little reshuffling of attitudes and priorities won't solve.

The reason a savings account often ends up on the short end of the budget is because that's where we tend to place savings—at the end.

Here's the secret to successful saving:

Instead of dishing out all your funds to your creditors and ending up with only lint in your pockets, *look upon yourself and your family as your number one creditor*. After tithe and taxes, try to designate a percentage of your take-home pay for personal savings *before paying any other bills*. This pay-yourself-first philosophy will thus guarantee that you'll be saving something every month, regardless of how much you owe to other people.

Pay yourself first!

Successful money managers usually try to save anywhere from 10 to 20 percent of their take-home pay, depending on how much they owe in installment debt. Those relatively debt-free can often afford to save close to 20 percent, perhaps even more if it doesn't choke their living expenses. For couples in heavy debt, financial counselors often recommend a plan similar to this one:

After tithe and taxes, designate:

10% *to savings and investment*
20% *to debt elimination* (No matter how much you owe, you can almost always legally arrange to lower and extend those monthly payments if necessary to meet your 20% limit)
70% *to living expenses* (In some cases, 70% may require an extra dose of self-discipline)

But deciding to pay yourself first is only half the savings strategy. Early in our marriage, Kathy and I found ourselves making two or three savings withdrawals for every deposit. There were just too many things we needed! What we struggled so hard to save seemed to disappear in just a few months.

As we talked about our finances, we came to realize that there was more than one purpose for saving. There is saving to *spend,* which we had been doing. It beats going hog-wild with credit cards, but it seems that every few months we had to start all over.

But then there is saving to *have.*

Have. That means an emergency fund for that possible unexpected lay-off, repair, accident, burglary, fire, or death. And for those whose company retirement plans are less than adequate (keep inflation in mind!) *having* also means a long-term fund for that blessed day of retirement.

So Kathy and I decided to divide our savings allotment into three separate accounts:

1. *A regular passbook account* (our *spend* account) in which we will save on a short-term basis for future needs such as lump insurance payments, down payments, a friend in need, a trip, Christmas, minor medical bills, etc.
2. *A higher-yield savings-and-loan account* in which we'll try to build up three or four months' emergency income

and let it draw interest until (if and when) we should need it.

3. *A tax-sheltered retirement fund* which, through the Keough Act, enables us to save for retirement without paying annual taxes on interest received. Taxes are deferred until we withdraw the funds after age 59, but presumably we will then be in a lower tax bracket.

The arrangement takes some patience, since our savings allotment goes into three funds instead of just one. But once the "emergency income" account reaches a level comparable to three or four months' income, we'll be able to contribute more to our short-term and retirement accounts. We like it, because it meets present-day needs while providing for the future.

Savings *are* important enough to be part of your fixed expenses. As you and your wife budget, place personal savings right up there with tithe, rent or mortgage, insurance, and all the rest of your fixed expenses.

Then comes the third question for budgeters:

What's left for our variable expenses? Subtract your total monthly fixed expenses from your total monthly income. The remainder is what you have available for variable (day-to-day) expenses.

Keep this figure handy, for you'll need it in answering the fourth and final budgeting question:

How can we most wisely spend that amount? This is where hundreds of couples get into trouble in family budgeting. They simply don't ask (and answer) this question.

Together, determine your monthly priorities in day-to-day spending.

Regular variable expenses will most likely include food, toiletries, utilities, transportation, home safety equipment, allowances, and recreation. These should be your cash priorities.

Then, depending upon the most immediate needs in a given month, *optional variable expenses* will include repairs and improvements, entertainment, furnishings, clothing, medical, postage and supplies, education, appliances, "fun" items. If you've made out your family priority list for spending, stick to it in administering your optional variable expenses.

Try to assign a specific cash figure to your regular variables. Utilities can be unpredictable, so estimate high on them. Then, by adding your total allotment for regular variable expenses to your total for fixed expenses, you'll be able to determine just how much is left each month for optional expenses (including installment purchases).

Your budget calculations can be summarized this way:

1. TOTAL MONTHLY INCOME

$$-\left(\begin{array}{c}\text{2. TOTAL FIXED EXPENSES}\\ \text{(Tithe, Savings, Taxes, Rent/Mortgage,}\\ \text{Insurance)}\\ +\\ \text{3. REGULAR VARIABLE EXPENSES}\\ \text{(Food, Utilities, Toiletries, Transportation,}\\ \text{Allowances, Recreation, Etc.)}\end{array}\right)$$

Monthly Amount Available for
4. OPTIONAL VARIABLE EXPENSES
(Clothing, Entertainment, Repairs, Improvements,
Medical, Postage, Furnishings, Etc.
Includes both cash purchases and
credit installment payments.)

Caution: Don't tie up all your remaining optional variable expense funds in credit purchases—you'll need the cash. Always keep in mind your Personal Debt Limit which you established earlier.

Now you have a complete listing of your monthly income and obligations. By indicating a date of the month on which payment is due on each obligation, you can divide your fixed and variable expenses between paychecks. Bills and needs during the first part of the month, for example, can be paid from a paycheck received on the 1st; expenses falling due during the latter part will be taken care of with the "15th" paycheck.

216

SAFEGUARD 5
When You're in Too Deep,
Admit It and Take Action.

If the day should ever come when you find yourself dog-paddling in debt, *don't* allow masculine pride, embarrassment, or fear of losing your credit rating keep you from seeking help. Putting off corrective action will only compound your problems.

First, admit to yourself that things are out of hand. Look back through your bills, check stubs, and savings withdrawals to try to spot unwise investments. Were they due to your direct spending, or your failure to communicate financial priorities to your wife and children? When you've admitted that you have a problem and accepted responsibility for it, you're ready for the next step.

Second, hold a family financial council on the budget. Until your children reach the teen years, this council would probably include just you and your wife. But as they become older and carry more responsibility, make finances a family affair. Be honest about the problem, and present it as an opportunity to work together as a team in solving it. Instead of presenting a mandatory cutback edict, challenge each family member to suggest ways in which to cut back on the allowances, "needs," and wants for awhile. Brainstorm together on a plan to get the family budget back in order.

With sensitive leadership, you can handle this meeting with a minimum of panic among the family. Of course, you'll need to determine ahead of time which children are old enough to contribute to, and benefit from, the experience. But don't gloss over the financial situation for your children. As Norman Lobsenz writes in a *Reader's Digest* article titled "Managing the Money Squeeze":

> As a rule, youngsters are better able to accept deprivations when their parents are frank about money

217

> problems. Observes a child psychologist: "Many parents confuse the giving of money or things with the giving of love. Children are better able than we realize to separate the two."

Present the facts with the confidence that things will work out if you all work together. Pray together, expecting God to give each of you wisdom and discipline. Seeing Dad admit a problem and work it out with Mom and the children will teach those kids an invaluable lesson—not only in financial responsibility, but in humility, communication, and leadership.

Where you go from there depends both on how long you've been dog-paddling and how deep the water. You may wish to put yourselves on the 10-20-70 system mentioned earlier, contacting each of your creditors and arranging to lessen the amount of your monthly installment payments. (To show that you're serious, tell them of your plan to pay them back and present it to them in writing. Keep a copy for yourself. As long as you are making a responsible effort to pay your debts, no creditor can legally require you to pay in terms higher than you can afford.)

If credit cards have been your downfall, simply take one pair of scissors, insert credit cards, and snip away until the cards are thoroughly shredded. You must still pay for what you've already bought, but you'll be protecting yourself from future impulses. Few stores will honor a pile of shredded plastic (and if you find one that does, you'd better double-check the quality of your purchase). Don't even *consider* applying for new cards until long after your present bills are paid off.

Whether you use the 10-20-70 plan or not, *do*—by all means—communicate with your creditors. Your silence will most likely convince them that you're trying to dodge your debt. On the other hand, if you show a genuine desire to get your finances in order, many will be patient with you. If, that is, you have taken the initiative to contact them before they have to phone *you*.

If your financial woes are even too much for self-imposed discipline to cure, then don't hesitate to get expert counseling.

Good financial counseling needn't cost you the $50-an-hour you'd have to shell out for a CPA or lawyer. There are a number of trustworthy, nonprofit credit-counseling services available in almost every section of the country. One of the best is the National Foundation for Consumer Credit, and by writing to their headquarters at 1819 "H" Street, NW, Washington, DC 20006, you can receive a list of their branch offices. The service costs are minimal, sometimes free. You'll also find your creditors to be more understanding if they know you're seeking good advice.

If you sense yourself flirting with financial bondage in any of its forms—debt, worry, or selfishness—I would encourage you to go back over these last two chapters and pinpoint any weak spots in your own personal attitudes toward money. Review the self-tests. Ask yourself if you've befriended some of the Money Monsters. Create opportunities, together with your wife and family, to sit down and reevaluate the priorities for your family budget.

Money is simply a tool for the provision of needs, the sharing of blessings with others, and the enjoyment of life. Never let it become more than that to you. But what you do have, manage with care. Resolve today that your goal in money management is not financial wealth, but something much greater: *financial freedom.*

18 Sex and the Raised Eyebrow

My darling bride is like a private garden that no one else can have, a fountain of my own.
KING SOLOMON,
Song of Solomon 4:12
(TLB)

Let him come into his garden and eat its choicest fruits.
THE WOMAN,
Song of Solomon 4:16
(TLB)

I have a sneaking hunch this is one of the first chapters you turned to.

If you did, you're just like me—and probably every other man with red blood in his veins. For us, the slightest hint of sex has always aroused curiosity.

Remember the awkward early years, when at age thirteen we first began noticing those strange sensations we couldn't understand? Suddenly, all the girls we had vowed to hate began to appeal to us. Maybe some questionable magazines began finding their way between the mattresses in our bedrooms. ("Can't figure out *how* they got there, Mom.") We began wondering what the real thing would be like someday.

But we didn't dare mention to anyone else what we were thinking. That little three-letter word had a way of causing raised eyebrows and awkward silences. So our sensual thoughts were kept private, very private. And questions were kept secret, very secret. We knew we shouldn't be thinking about such things—why couldn't we be normal, like all the other boys?

What we didn't realize was that the other boys were going through just the same thing. We've learned quite a bit since those pubescent years. We're older, more mature. As husbands, we know what the real thing is like. But our curiosity and imagination haven't faded a bit: The questions are from a deeper perspective, that's all.

Some husbands are dealing with the moral questions that might be involved in certain sexual attitudes and techniques. Some feel uncomfortable—even to the point of impotency—when their wives display sexual aggressiveness. Others are realizing for the first time that their knowledge of female sexual response, if written in book form, might fill the back of a postage stamp. And some just want to make a great thing in their marriages even greater.

So there's probably no better way to begin a trilogy on How to Keep a Woman Sexually Satisfied than to deal with some of the basic questions men think about but are often afraid to ask. In the following pages, we'll look at twelve of the most common ones.

"What is the real purpose of sex—procreation or pleasure?"

Foundationally, neither one. The primary purpose of sexual union is to symbolize the oneness of body, mind, and spirit that is to take place when a man marries a woman. In Genesis 2 God presented Adam with Eve. Verse 24 says, "This explains why [in the marriage of man and woman] a man leaves his father and mother, and is joined to his wife in such a way that the two become one person" (TLB).

Fortunately, God had two delightful fringe benefits in mind for this symbolic act. One of these established sex as the means of procreation of children. *But it did not limit sex strictly to this purpose.* Throughout history, and even in some present-day circles, some well-intentioned people have regarded sex for reasons other than conception as indulgent, and therefore evil. We've all read about the board that extended down the middle of some beds to waylay any thoughts of hanky-panky. There is even one early account of a Puritan husband who delivered his wife up for execution because she had actually *smiled* during intercourse.

Such legalism is a tragic misinterpretation of a gift given to marriages by a loving God. If he intended sex to be strictly utilitarian (once, and only once, for each child you are to raise), it is doubtful that he would have made the sexual urges so strong, or made the organs themselves so sensitive to arousal, or made the sexual climax feel so *good*.

The very design and beauty of the entire sexual system makes the chief fringe benefit of the sex act obvious: enjoyment. Sex is intended for pleasure and no married couple should feel pangs of guilt if they find themselves enjoying it "too much."

"Can you show me evidence that God intended sex for pleasure?"

The man and woman depicted in Song of Solomon weren't exactly discussing the waxy yellow buildup on the linoleum. Indeed, the entire eight chapters of this biblical love story are a wholehearted endorsement of conjugal eroticism. The language may be a bit more flowery than we would use today, but the basic message is the same: "I love you. You turn me on. I want to make love to you."

And back in Genesis we see God standing over all that he had created. It was at the end of the sixth day, when he made man and woman. "And God saw *all* that he had made," the account reads, "and, behold, it was *very good*" [italics mine]. "All" included those sex organs with their ultrasensitive nerve endings and boundless capacity for marvelous sensations.

The fifth chapter of Proverbs minces no words about sexual pleasure in marriage. In the midst of a convincing entreaty on the need for husbands to be faithful, we find these words: "Let your manhood be a blessing; *rejoice* in the wife of your youth. Let her charms and tender embrace *satisfy* you. Let her love alone *fill you with delight*" (Proverbs 5:18, 19, TLB) [italics mine].

Then, in addition to declaring sex "very good" and adjuring men to "rejoice" in their wives, *God demands that the husband and wife satisfy each other.* "The man should give his wife all that is her right as a married woman," we read in 1 Corinthians 7:3-5 (TLB), "and the wife should do the same for her husband: for a girl who marries no longer has full right to her own body, for her husband then has his rights to it, too; and in the same way the husband no longer has full right to his own body, for it belongs also to his wife. So do not refuse these rights to each other."

People tend to overreact when they hear the very few guidelines which God *has* placed on sex. Many have wrongly concluded that "God is down on sex." But nothing could be further from the truth: He thought it all up. And when he did, he probably had a big smile on his face.

"You seem to take a pretty relaxed attitude about it ..."

You bet. For too many husbands and wives, sex has become something you do but don't talk about. I agree that we should be discreet about discussing marital sensuality—but with each other?

The sexual relationship is so important to a good marriage that a couple *must* be relaxed about it—relaxed enough to talk freely about what does and doesn't excite them. Some men go through an entire marriage thinking, "I wish she'd do such-and-such to me during foreplay, but if I asked her, she'd think I'm a pervert...." Their wives, at the same time, may be thinking, "I sure would like it if we did such-and-such together, but he might think I have a dirty mind."

Then, too, each may be *doing* something that the other person doesn't enjoy at all. How are they going to know what fulfills their spouse if they are unable to talk about it?

A couple must also be relaxed enough about sex to laugh about it. If you and your mate try a new position and feel more like a hot soft pretzel than the sensuous couple, have a good laugh together!

And if you can't achieve an erection tonight, don't make the mistake of taking it too seriously. Since almost every man suffers temporary impotencies due to anxiety or fatigue, an occasional droop is nothing to worry about. Laugh about it together, and look forward to the next time. Many "permanent" impotencies are caused by a communication breakdown after one or two of these temporary disappointments. Silent brooding only increases anxiety and compounds the pressure on the husband to "perform." Soon, he may give up trying altogether, simply because the couple took that initial "failure" so seriously.

Sex is a gradual learning experience—a "twenty year warmup," as Dr. Charlie Shedd has aptly described it. Let the learning process—with all its victories, inevitable dry spells and mistakes—provoke joy instead of tears. Sex is something worth being relaxed about!

"How often is normal?"

This seems to be an especially intriguing question to new bridegrooms who want to make sure that they match up to, or surpass, the national average. "How often?" might also plague the husband who has been wed several years and finds it necessary to bolster his sense of manhood.

The liberating truth is that *whatever pleases you and your wife is normal.* Whether you make love once a day or once a month, the frequency of coitus was never intended to be a gauge of manliness or virility.

There is no reason for you to let anyone else's standards invade the privacy of your bedroom. The only important criterion is: Are *both of you* satisfied with the frequency of your sexual embraces? If so, fine. That's the only standard you need.

"How much time should it take?"
How much time do you *have?*

You can "have intercourse" in two to five minutes (and unfortunately, there are many couples who do). This may be long enough to relieve an overly eager husband, but forget satisfying the wife in this amount of time. Better yet, forget five-minute sex altogether.

Good sex takes as long as is necessary to bring both the husband and wife to climax. *Great* sex will take even longer.

"It bothers me when my wife becomes sexually aggressive. Isn't this the man's role?"
We men don't exactly have a monopoly on sexual desire and imagination. The only way to explain the phenomenal sales of *The Sensuous Woman,* books by Masters and Johnson, *The Total Woman,* and *The Joy of Sex* is to realize that women have at last begun feeling free enough to admit that they want (and *need*) sensual excitement and adventure.

Let's face it—our women have been reading up. They're discovering their vast potential for sexual enjoyment—a potential that their husbands might not be fulfilling as of yet. And the more they learn, the more entitled they feel (and rightly so) to their God-given rights of life, liberty, and the pursuit of multiple orgasms.

There are some men whose masculinity is so wrapped up in societal roles that wifely aggression deeply disturbs them. There is no reason for the husband to be resentful, or to feel inadequate, if his wife initiates sexual seduction and aggressiveness. In fact, he should learn to look on it as a blessing, for female sexual assertiveness can be downright tantalizing.

It's interesting to note that for the *clitoris,* that tiny

female organ capable of producing explosions of ecstasy, modern medicine has been able to find no other function than that of female pleasure. Our wives were obviously made to be sexually titillated and fulfilled—and research has also shown that their capacity for sexual climax is far greater than ours.

So the husband who does not exercise the love and self-control necessary to satisfy his wife is only cheating her. And if her being aggressive is part of her sensuality, he needn't feel jeopardized, but should rejoice that his woman is so sexually alive.

"I've read some glorified accounts of how long the penis ought to be for maximum sensation in the woman, but mine doesn't measure up to anything near that. What's the truth about penis size?"

"The bigger the better" is misleading. Actually, size has little to do with satisfying sex, and the truth is that men with giant sex organs are more the exception than the rule. The pornography market has generated countless myths about the necessity of the enormous penis, and it's time we set the record straight.

Research has shown that the penis, in its relaxed state, varies in length from man to man, but the average is between two and three inches. Erect, nearly all are six to seven inches in length. This is more than enough to provide excellent penetration and stimulation of your partner, for only the first two to three inches of her vagina respond significantly to penile stimulation.

So there's no need to feel short-changed—all of us have been blessed with more than enough to achieve the desired result.

"Which sex acts are OK, and which are morally wrong?"

This question invariably rates a raised eyebrow, for whenever you deal in specifics there's bound to be controversy. But if you're married and irrevocably committed to each other, you can breathe easy when it comes to what's right and wrong in the bedroom. The One who created sex has given you a free rein.

The Bible specifies only four sexual acts as sin before God, and all of them involve sex with someone (or something) other than your spouse: *homosexuality*—sex with a person of your own gender; *bestiality*—sex with an animal; *fornication*—sex between unmarried persons of opposite sexes; and *adultery*—sex with a married person other than your spouse.

Within your marriage, however, God's Word places no restriction on foreplay or intercourse. You and your wife have complete freedom of arousal. In his excellent cassette study album entitled "Sex Problems and Sex Techniques in Marriage," Dr. Ed Wheat states, "There is no wrongness in married sex, as long as the husband or the wife do not offend each other or give a sense of discomfort to each other." The album, with its thorough presentation of medical and biblical guidelines, is endorsed by several prominent Christian leaders and marriage counselors.

Feel free to be creative together! Any private act which you and your spouse *both enjoy* in seduction, sex play, and sexual intercourse is morally sound. You're limited only by your imaginations and personal tastes.

"What about the use of erotic movies and photographs to stimulate mutual eagerness?"

On the plus side, some psychologists feel that if a husband and wife are having a difficult time both doing and talking about sex, the viewing of explicit movies and photographs may help to open the doors of arousal and communication for them.

But, most add, such visual stimulation has only a temporary value.

Knowing how men tend to respond to erotic portrayals

prompts me to counsel against such a practice. Rather than bringing about the desired effect (increased longing for sex with your wife), watching another couple go at it on film will more likely induce adulterous fantasy (desire for the woman in the film or photograph). Mental adultery doesn't do your marriage a bit of good.

You and your wife will have far more fun creating your *own* eroticism, as we'll see in the next chapter.

"The other day I heard that husbands should be just as concerned about sex hygiene as their wives. What should I be aware of?"

Sex hygiene for men can be summed up in those three magic words: Wash your penis. Regular, thorough bathing of the genitals is essential not only for a pleasant smell, but to aid in preventing diseases such as penile and prostate cancer (in you) and cervical cancer (in her).

Be especially certain to cleanse the area just under the head of the penis, as this is where bacteria and impurities find it easy to accumulate.

"I recognize that a woman needs to be fulfilled sexually, but I'm finding that it's not as simple as it sounds. What all is involved in meeting my wife's sexual needs?"

The more you get to know that woman of yours, the more you'll realize that she has a set of sexual turn-ons which are almost unique to her personality. One of your most challenging and enjoyable quests in life should be to discover just the right atmospheres, moods, words, clothing, attitudes, etc., that excite her—and to provide those as much as you can.

There's one thing of which you can be certain: The variety of sexual intercourse in which the husband is through within five minutes is nothing but animal selfishness. The educated wife of today won't stand for it, and you should be ashamed if that's been your style.

Meeting your wife's physical needs requires a lifelong commitment on your part to *give* enjoyment as well as to receive it. One way to keep the home fires burning is through creative seduction, or The Art of Making the Trip to the Bedroom as Full of Ecstasy as Possible. The other way is to know what to do once you get her there.

To these goals—and to her sexual happiness—the following two chapters are dedicated.

19
Turn-Offs and Turn-Ons

"Kiss me again and again, for your love is sweeter than wine. How fragrant your cologne, and how great your name! No wonder all the young girls love you! Take me with you; come, let's run!"
THE WOMAN,
Song of Solomon
1:2-4 (TLB)

I'm becoming convinced that the average American male could probably have sex and reach climax right in the middle of a bitter argument, an air raid, or *Jaws*. When that urge strikes us, the mood and surrounding circumstances may make little difference.

We men can often isolate sex from other emotions by placing it in one of life's many "compartments": There is a time for work. A time for relaxation. A time for eating. A time for worship. A time for pleasure. We act when our schedules, or our human drives, call for a certain activity.

But for a woman, sex follows a different pattern of order. She tends to look at sexuality as an integral part of her entire being. Successful sex, to her, is more than just the experience of orgasm—*it is the total setting of intimacy surrounding her marriage.*

Your wife's most important sex organ is not genital. Her most vital sex organ is

231

her mind. If your relationship together is one of intimacy, communication, and love, her mind tells her "All systems are GO!"—sexual abandonment with you will make her joy even more complete. But if something is wrong elsewhere in the marriage, you can bet it will put a damper on her sexual outlook.

And for the same reason, the *setting and mood* from which you initiate sexual union is crucial to her. While the husband may be able to move straight from that bitter argument to sexual intimacy (it always works in the movies), her mind will be saying, "You've got to be kidding." Sex for her must be born from an atmosphere of love and tenderness.

The husband who continually demonstrates his love, and then takes the time to properly set the mood (even when things have been going great), will provide far greater sexual fulfillment for the woman he married—and for himself.

Setting the right mood is what this chapter is about. With a little common sense and creative thinking, you can help make seduction and intercourse a delightful adventure for her.

But before we get to the specifics, let's pause a moment. Some of us are blowing the whole thing before the party even begins.

Before we explore some of the things that turn a woman on, we'd better consider some definite sexual turn-*offs,* suggested with conviction by several experienced wives. These items might seem slight to us, and perhaps that's why many of us violate them. But you can be sure that they're high on your wife's list of Things That Throw Cold Water on Sex Before We Even Get Started. If we don't use our heads, our attempts at playing Casanova will be about as provocative to her as the Consumer Price Index.

What Turns
a Woman Off?

Keep in mind some of these common atrocities:

B. O. and bad breath. If she's been swooning in your presence, it might not be your suaveness. Perhaps she's trying to give you a hint. Body odor affects her sex drive like an ice-cold shower affects yours, so don't expect smooth seduction with dried volleyball sweat or a breath that could knock out Muhammad Ali.

Scratchy chin. (In sex, also known as prickly heat.) To get an idea of how sexy beard stubble can be, just scrape a piece of No. 12 sandpaper back and forth across your face. Unless she has given you the OK to grow a full, soft beard, keep the chin smooth for her. How would you like it if she took a Brillo pad to *your* face?

Wandering eyes. Husband and wife are out together, on the beach, in a restaurant, or wherever other women are to be found, and he can't help looking them over with obvious appreciation. Sometimes he even expresses some of his sentiments aloud. Later, he can't figure out why his wife isn't eager to ease his red-hot desires. Truth is, she's not the least bit interested in surrogate sex.

The Greaser. Running fingers through his hair is not unlike fondling Crisco. The Greaser either ignores shampooing for three or four days and lets the stuff accumulate, or else he's still using the pomades and creams and oils that spilled forth from his TV tube in the 1950s.

The wet look isn't at all necessary in this day of dry hairsprays and hand-held styling dryers for men, and for most women the human oil slick is enough to call out the Environmental Protection Agency.

The Mauler. He attempts to show love, but definitely at the wrong time. I've been guilty of this one on several occasions, when Kathy and I are about to go out and she has spent an entire hour fixing her hair, outfit, and makeup.

"You look beautiful!" I exclaim. So far so good. My compliment pleases her. Then, forever debonair, I wrap my arms around her and plant a full, passionate kiss on those sweet lips.

Her smile falters. In one fell swoop I've managed to crush her hair, wrinkle her clothes, and smear her lip gloss. The only thing "cool" about the situation is the icy look in her eyes as she returns to the mirror for repairs.

Cold. The almost unanimous consensus among women is that in sex, *they can't stand cold.* So if you have some jolly ideas for later on and she's mentioned that she feels chilly, put another log on the fire, quick.

The Brat. Every wife has, at some time or another, found herself married to one. The Brat starts making grabs as soon as he feels the urge, but if she is incapable of excitement at that particular moment, he'll whine, demand, pout, sulk, throw tantrums, and hold his breath until he turns blue. The Brat's favorite line is "After I put in a hard day at the office to feed and clothe you, the least you can do is *give* a little." Occasionally his ploy succeeds, but only for a morose moment of one-way sex. *She* might find more excitement at a wake.

Bad timing. Closely akin to The Mauler and The Brat, the husband with a tendency toward bad timing doesn't realize the importance of setting the mood beforehand. His passions strike just as the lasagna is spilling over in the oven, or as Junior is reproducing the Mona Lisa in crayon on the bathroom wall, or twenty minutes before the Ladies' Auxiliary is due for tea and cookies. If the urge hits in times like these, it might be more advisable to try fifteen quick pushups.

Rough hands. Like beard stubble, rough and calloused hands can make foreplay more like dermabrasion surgery. Your hands are important tools in sexual stimulation, and it is not at all unmasculine to keep them soft for her with regular use of a good hand lotion. While you're at it, check those fingernails. Keeping them trimmed and clean is essential for the intimate moments.

Well, these are a few of the basic turn-offs to watch out for. Some close communication between you and your lover may bring out others, and that's good. In addition, you'll probably gain some insight on what *does* excite her. That's even better.

What Turns
a Woman On?

As we pointed out in the last chapter, every woman has her own unique turn-ons, and the more you share together in sensual discovery the more you'll learn about how to arouse and fulfill your wife's sexual appetite.

But there are several things husbands can do that are almost universal in their sex appeal for women. If you were to ask your wife about them, she would probably say, "Yes, by all means, I *like* that!" But don't ask her: Surprise her. Remember that for her sex includes the total setting of intimacy surrounding your coming together. Be creative. Take time to set the mood. You may find you've married a tigress.

What turns a woman on?

The man who meets her womanly needs. One of the best ways you can prepare for carefree sex is to make the meeting of her emotional needs a top priority from Day One of your marriage.

Why? Well, have you ever tried making love while the tea kettle is whistling? Distracting, right? Especially for her. Before she can lose herself in your masculine embrace, she's got to get up and take care of that thing in the kitchen.

It's just the same when things aren't quite right in your relationship. If there's a disagreement that hasn't been talked out and forgiven, or if you've been miserly with the encouragement and understanding, sex is the last thing on her mind. Those weak spots in the relationship are too distracting to her. Before having sex with you she wants to know that all of life's in good order.

Try to be meeting all of those womanly needs we discussed earlier—not as a "what'll-you-give-me-in-return?" gesture but motivated by sincere, unselfish *love*. Fulfilling her emotionally is the first step toward fulfilling her sexually.

The sharp dresser. It's a rare woman who doesn't appreciate—and get somewhat excited about—the man who

235

garbs himself in neat, up-to-date clothing. This doesn't mean you have to blow half a year's salary to look like a model from *Gentleman's Quarterly*. Just do the very best with what you *can* afford. Shop for pants, shirts, and jackets that go together in a variety of coordinates. Keep your eye open for the sales at good men's stores. And if you really want to please her, take her along to help you shop.

Remember: Nice clothing on hubby is exciting to her. Find out what turns her on by asking her to point out the men's styles she especially likes.

Cleanliness. "The best sex aids ever invented," one wife told me, "are soap, toothpaste, deodorant, and shampoo." Every wife interviewed agreed with her. "What turns me on?" another began. "Well, among other things, an aura of cleanliness. I may sound like a commercial, but I want him to look and smell fresh. If he doesn't, forget it. Send him to the showers."

We are dealing, men, with a delicate sense of smell that is often far more sensitive than our own. Have you ever noticed your wife flitting through the house, sniffing at the air and saying, "What's that smell?" And you replied, *"What* smell?" In my own household, Kathy can smell the salami in the refrigerator (from another room) every time I open the refrigerator door. I can't smell it if it's sitting on my upper lip.

A woman's acute sense of smell, combined with her innate urge for cleanliness, can detect an all-day armpit long before we even begin to make our move.

But she can also pick up the freshness that comes with the daily shower (or two), the brushing of teeth after meals (topped off by a mouthwash rinse), the protection of a good deodorant *(ask* her if yours is doing the job), and the clean, grease-free hair that results from regular shampooing. We husbands will spend a full half-hour preparing ourselves to *leave* her in the morning; why not invest a few minutes at the end of the work day to prepare for *coming home* to her? We can make that welcome-home hug a much more enjoyable experience for her by keeping a small cache of cologne, deodorant, and breath freshener at the office for late afternoon touch-ups (our fellow employees probably won't mind, either).

Women aren't merely pacified by cleanliness; they are attracted to it. It's worth all the time it takes.

Romance. Ongoing romance is so important to a good marriage that we've made a whole chapter out of it ("101 Ways to Make Your Wife Feel Like That Special Woman"). But, if you get my meaning, there is a time for romance, and there is a time for Romance.

When you sense that the mood is right for a torrid evening together, send the kids with Uncle Arthur across town and plan a private candlelight dinner "at our place." If she *wants* to fix a nice dinner, fine; otherwise, give her a vacation from the kitchen by either fixing dinner yourself or bringing something home. The cuisine isn't nearly as important as the mood.

After some relaxed dining, conversation, and background music, dessert is the time for that intimate little gift. Better stores everywhere are filled with all kinds of things you can buy to assure her that deep down, you're still hot for her. You might present her with the sauciest bikini underwear you can find. Or a slinky nightgown with a neckline that would make Cher blush. Or a see-through blouse for wearing "just at home." You may render her speechless for the first time in your marriage, but she'll love the gift. So will you.

And your thoughtfulness needn't be expensive. Even a special card, love note, or single flower will get the message through to her: She's special. She's your favorite person. And her closeness is desirable now—even more than ever before.

Then, make love to her with your words (this can start in the afternoon with a phone call from the office). Tell her how much you've missed her during the day. That you love her. That she's beautiful. How great it is to be alone with her. What she means to you. And if she's in a particularly graphic mood, tell her exactly what you'd like to do with her later on.

Marya Mannes wrote that "All really great lovers are articulate, and verbal seduction is the surest road to actual seduction." That line, gentlemen, is written for us by a woman.

The natural aphrodisiacs. By natural aphrodisiacs, we mean those simple things that can appeal so much to a woman's sensuality:

A liberal splash of men's cologne on your neck (by now you probably know her favorites)

Soft, unbuttonable clothing (on her and on you)

Burning incense (you can get several sticks for a quarter in most gift shops. Just be sure to burn it in a safe place or the evening may get hotter than you'd planned.)

Soft lighting (there's something mystical about candlelight and fireplaces)

Background music *(soft instrumental*—save Madame Butterfly and Great Hymns of Faith for some other evening)

Fresh flowers (you might have them delivered during the afternoon)

The spirit of sexual adventure. Happy is the married couple who discover together that variety is the spice of life, especially sex life. Never underestimate your woman on this one. She may be more adventuresome than you think.

Like men, most women are excited by a sense of the *risque* in married sex, as long as the adventure is *tasteful.* This rules out infidelity and cruelty in any of their forms, and for practical reasons you might also want to forget doing it on your mother-in-law's kitchen table or standing up in a canoe. But keeping good taste in your sexual adventure still leaves a lot of room for creativity.

What have you both always wanted to do together but

been hesitant to bring up? The best way to find out is to discuss it together some evening when the lights are low and the libido is high. (If you've ever wondered what is meant by "stimulating conversation," you won't wonder much longer.)

Along with the tantalizing fantasies you both come up with, you may want to consider a few settings and ideas which couples have been enjoying down through the ages:

Different times, different places. If you find yourselves locked into a sex-by-the-schedule routine (only at bedtime, only in our bed), do yourselves a favor and break free once in awhile. See if you can clear the house (and lock the doors) for some good old daytime sex on the couch or living room carpet. Or let the carpet (complemented with some fluffy pillows) serve as your bed after that seductive candlelight dinner together. As much as possible, let spontaneity rule when it comes to the time and place for sex.

The sensuous couple is almost always turned on even further at the sight of a motel room. It would be interesting to do a psychological study of this phenomenon, but whether a motel room reminds them of their honeymoon or lets them imagine a clandestine arrangement, such a break from the usual can be fun (and good for the heart).

So sometime soon, make a date with your wife for a sizzling, X-rated weekend vacation at a nice motel.

As you both look forward to it, help each other select and pack the outfits, underwear, and colognes that appeal to each other the most. Make it a point to clear your schedule so you'll be totally relaxed and hassle-free during the time together. Don't forget those special touches: some incense, candles, and perhaps a portable FM radio. And—if you can afford the moderate investment—surprise your lover with an extra-special aphrodisiac: satin. In finer department stores you can find satin sheets and pillow cases in any color from flaming pink to shiny black.

Clothing on, Clothing off. The porno-story image of the man ripping the woman's blouse from her back is a bit unrealistic. For one thing, your wife can't afford for you to rip

her blouses to shreds with every seduction. But most important, she craves the d-e-l-i-c-i-o-u-s-l-y s-l-o-w stimulation
that begins first with thoughts and romance, then proceeds
through intimate glances, gentle touches, sensual disrobing,
generous foreplay, and the climax itself.

As you begin to undress and explore her, she may do the
same with you. Let her, for now visual as well as tactile
arousal is filling her consciousness.

The nude human body, properly cared for, is one of the
most beautiful creations imaginable. But sometimes just the
right article of clothing (or absence of it) can make the
spouse's imagination run wild.

In bed, clothing needn't always be completely discarded.
Occasionally, you'll both enjoy continuing the imagination
game throughout intercourse by leaving on the unbuttoned
shirt or blouse, jewelry (though watches and rings can
scratch the skin or snag hair) or other select items of apparel. Sensual clothing is a matter of such personal taste
that you should feel free to express your likes and dislikes to
each other.

Multiple roles. Variety in sex goes beyond the mechanics
of "positions" to the identity your wife may wish to assume
once you have begun foreplay. One evening, she may wish to
be "conquered"—totally submissive to your aggressiveness;
on another occasion she may feel like the dominant
tigress—ravenous for your body and unafraid to show it; and
in a third encounter, she may desire an in-between identity
where both she and you are equally submissive and dominant in turning each other on. All three roles can be exciting
to her if you'll allow her to freely express herself with you.

Etcetera. The ideas for intimate sexual adventure are limited only by your personal imaginations and tastes. Some
couples highly recommend sharing the soap bubbles in the
bath or shower, and others swear by an occasional interlude
of music and colored light bulbs. Whatever setting you
choose, be sure that it is something *both of you* enjoy. That
touch of the risque should never become a sensual end in
itself, but merely a means of helping intensify your desire

for fulfilling each other.

I realize that some may regard a few of the above ideas as a bit too much. Then, too, when you and your wife begin to come up with your *own* ideas, these might be rated "G" by comparison. The important thing is for us to realize that our wives do have sexual cravings and imagination, and that we can better satisfy their adventurous spirits by taking the lead in communication and creativity.

There is one more item in our study of "What Turns a Woman On." Too many men ignore it; some, believe it or not, are even unaware of it. It is perhaps the greatest physical thrill we can provide for her: the orgasm. It can make the rest of the seduction seem like a Sunday on Sunnybrook Farm.

That's why it deserves a whole chapter of its own.

20 Fulfilling Your Woman

"His left hand is under my head and with his right hand he embraces me."
THE WOMAN,
Song of Solomon 2:6
(TLB)

Now comes the moment (or if things go well, the hour) of truth. You've created the mood, set the stage, and whispered sweet somethings in her ear. She's ready and willing. You're ready and willful. So far, it's been a sumptuous evening.

Now maybe sex in a mirrored bedroom isn't one of the fantasies you and your wife have agreed upon, but let's imagine for a moment. Say you've installed a giant mirror on the ceiling just above your bed. As you, El Suavo, proceed to make love with your wife, would you see:

a. A man whose love is so strong for her that meeting *her* sexual needs comes first? or

b. A man more interested in playing "Beat the Clock"—and whose selfishness or clumsiness (or both) leaves her frustrated and unsatisfied?

Sex can be very revealing, and by that I mean of more than just the flesh and genitalia. The way you go about sexual intercourse with your woman has an un-

243

canny way of unveiling the true quality of the everyday love you hold for her.

Now be honest. What did the mirrors reveal—is your love in the marriage bed a self-centered type of love that says, in effect, "Me first"? Or does the love you hold for your wife motivate you to give her the sensual fulfillment she needs?

It has been said that there is no such thing as a frigid woman—only a clumsy man. Of course there are exceptions, but a tragic number of unhappy marriages today bear out that statement. Selfishness or ignorance on the part of the husband *can* eventually drive the woman to literal aversion to sexual contact.

The key to preventing such marital misery is twofold: First, make sure that genuine *agape* love rules your heart—even in the bedroom. *Agape* is that unabashed brand of love which finds just as much pleasure in giving as in receiving. Teamed up with some skilled *eros* (the sensual love), *agape* is guaranteed to take the selfishness out of sex.

Second, know what pleases your wife in sexual stimulation—*and do it.* As in all phases of the seduction, she'll have her own little secrets as to what-and-when best prepares her for orgasm, and for this reason it's important to know the *person,* not just the method.

But, as in seduction, there are also some basic principles of female sexual response on which most women agree. To adequately explore these principles we'll look at the sex act in each of its five phases.

THE FIRST PHASE
Preparation

What needs to be readied? Primarily, *her mind.* If you've employed some of the suggestions in the last chapter, you're already well into the preparation phase of successful sex. *Do take the time to prepare her!* Make her transition from everyday thinking to erotic thoughts as breathtaking as possible. This will determine whether her mind is on you or on tomorrow's dinner menu.

One thing which almost every woman desires when making love is the assurance of privacy. Close the bedroom door behind you and lock it securely. (Children need to learn to respect a closed door as a normal aspect of family privacy.) You can provide low lighting in the boudoir by either bringing the lighted candles in with you, or by installing a simple rheostat device in your light fixtures *(don't,* however, take the time to install one *now).* And now, more than any other moment, is the time to take that phone off the hook. There is nothing more anti-climactic than having the chairwoman of the church bake sale call just as things are starting to perk up.

It can never be emphasized enough that the skillful seducer prepares his wife *slowly but progressively* for their time together. This is especially true in that heart-thumping moment when preparation turns into ...

THE SECOND PHASE
Foreplay

This is the phase, gentlemen, that makes or breaks the female orgasm. Approach it with a generous spirit.

The all-important watchword in foreplay is *tenderness.* It implies an ongoing communication between the two of you as to what excites and what detracts from arousal. Tenderness excludes the wild grabbing and squeezing of breasts and other erogenous areas, as well as the misplaced elbow. As her level of rapture increases, the pressure administered can be gradually increased—especially to the clitoris—but not at first. Enter foreplay with all the tenderness of word and touch that got you both there in the first place.

Your ultimate objective in foreplay is to stimulate the *clitoris*—her tiny, sensitive, erectile organ found just below the foreskin of her vulva.

The clitoris is the female equivalent to the male penis,

245

which should tell you quite a bit about how it responds to proper stimulation. Though it does not ejaculate, it does become engorged through stimulation and somewhat enlarged with sexual arousal, and it is the key to her orgasm.

But don't make the mistake of moving to the ultimate objective right away. Without sufficient pre-arousal, the vulva and clitoris can be too sensitive to the touch and your haste might cause more discomfort than joy.

The husband seeking the ideal model of sensuous foreplay can't go wrong with the quotation that leads off this chapter: "His left hand is under my head," the woman in Song of Solomon is saying, "and with his right hand he embraces me." The husband is apparently lying on his side next to his wife, where he can easily fondle her with his right hand. The wife, on her back, has both hands free to caress her husband's penis. The idea is a good one, allowing for all kinds of possibilities in mutual stimulation.

Practically every inch of the female body responds to the loving touch, but there are several "erogenous zones" that can especially excite her. Use that free hand to *gently and slowly* embrace these areas as you work your way down to the clitoris:

The eyelids. When her eyes are closed and your hands are at work elsewhere, brush her eyelids softly with kisses. A favorite (and one which usually evokes a small chuckle) is the "butterfly kiss"—done not with the lips but with the eyelash. Just flick your eyelashes up and down on her closed eyelids, and you'll see what I mean.

The ears and earlobes. For some women, this is more funny-ticklish than libido-ticklish, so be sure your wife tells you how it affects her. The popular "breathe in my ear and I'll follow you anywhere" statement smacks of sexual overtones for a very good reason: When she hears (and feels) the mounting excitement in your breathing, that frenzy goes right down her ear canal to her brain. If she seems to like it, combine the ear-nuzzling with light nibbles and flicks of the tongue on her earlobe.

The mouth. You'll want to return to this erogenous

zone throughout the foreplay and intercourse. Gentleness is still the vogue, though as passions rise her lips can handle greater expression from yours. Be sure to always cushion your lips against hers to avoid skewering her with your teeth. *Never* peck at her as if you were late for the office; nor should you hold a kiss so long she can't breathe. Combine gentle soft kisses with longer firm ones.

The neck. Breathing, butterfly flicks, and gentle kisses here will give her sensations similar to those around the ear.

The breasts. Women vary in the amount of satisfaction they derive from breast stimulation, but most agree that this is one area where the husband will find it worthwhile to linger. While I do not agree with all of Dr. Alex Comfort's views, his passage on "Breasts" in *The Joy of Sex* gives us an insight into one woman's opinion:

> She says: "Men still don't understand about breasts, or are in too much of a hurry to get lower down—unlike a man's nipples, a woman's have a direct hot line to her clitoris.... Palm-brushing, eyelid-brushing, licking ... can work wonders; the orgasms one gets from these are mind-blowing, without detracting a jot from intercourse to come after. *Please take time.*"

The tummy. Give it a light massage and gentle kiss on your way down to ...

... The thighs. Where soft kisses and handwork, slowly alternating from the inside of one thigh to the inside of the other, will make her shudder with delight. Gradually, increase your flirtations with the lips of her vulva by circling around the area and brushing lightly with your fingers. After several minutes, her clitoris should be panting for direct stimulation. The simplest way to locate it is by placing your palm on her stomach, fingers down, and then sliding your hand downward until your middle finger descends over the center of the foreskin. With just a slight amount of pressure, you'll feel the stiffened shaft of the clitoris with

the tip of your finger. (If you have trouble finding it, have your wife guide your hand with hers.)

Experience will tell you just how much pressure and manipulation best suits your wife's wishes, but one beautiful thing about the clitoris is that it has a much higher pain threshold than the male's penis. Some women prefer softness here, too; but most respond best to a firm, back-and-forth (side to side) stimulation by the finger.

One important rule, however: Avoid continuing the same kind of finger manipulation over a length of time, as the clitoris can become numb from too much of a good thing. You can keep it lubricated by occasionally dipping your fingers down into the mouth of the vagina, where her body will by this time be manufacturing its own lubricating fluid.

Dr. Comfort points out a further technique to help prepare her for orgasm, which in some women may bring even more intense pleasure (but be sure to first discuss this with your wife and gently "experiment" a little):

> For preparation as well as orgasm, the flat of the hand on the vulva with the middle finger between the lips, and its tip moving in and out of the vagina, while the ball of the palm presses hard just above the pubis, is probably the best method. Steady rhythm is the most important thing, taking it from her hip movements...

You can bring your lover to orgasm through the skilled use of clitoral/vaginal stimulation alone (remember this if you *should* ejaculate prematurely, or for giving her two or three orgasms to your one). The inserted penis is not really that necessary for clitoral arousal, for there is considerable space between the vaginal opening and the clitoris. The husband who is perplexed because he has trouble stimulating his wife's clitoris with his penis can rest assured that he is not "abnormal" in some way. Fact is, the penis is about as effective as the kneecap. That's one reason why the Master Designer put "... and with his right *hand* he embraces me" in the guidebook.

248

Intimate verbal communication should never cease during foreplay and intercourse, though it's understandable that your words may gradually become more exclamatory than subdued. But continue to assure her—as best as a frenzied mind can—that you love her, love her body, love this time together. She should feel free to express the same sentiments to you, as well as assorted technical information to let you know when you're stimulating the right spots.

As we'll soon see, verbal communication also plays a vital role in each of the remaining three phases.

THE THIRD PHASE
Entry

There is only one proper time for you to insert your erect penis into her vagina, and that's *when she is ready for it.* Entering her before she is sufficiently aroused can cause her some discomfort due to dryness, and will also make premature ejaculation on your part more likely. Agree ahead of time that she will inform you when she's mentally and physically prepared for insertion.

THE FOURTH PHASE
Orgasm

There has long been a myth hovering over the marriage bed that truly satisfying sex can only occur upon *simultaneous orgasm*—in which both the man and wife reach orgasm at the same instant. The truth is that, while simultaneous orgasm is pleasant, it is not at all necessary for total fulfillment. Nor is it as probable as some would have us believe.

The goal to strive for in sexual intercourse is *mutual orgasm*—in which both husband and wife experience that distinct sexual release. In order to achieve that goal, you'll perhaps want to review a few basics about how the female responds.

249

Much more is known about the male orgasm than that of the female. When we reach orgasm, we have an ejaculation of seminal fluid which, if not contained within the vagina, would be projected from twelve to twenty-four inches. Accompanying ejaculation is an almost violent muscle spasm, which culminates in strong pelvic thrusts. After orgasm, it will take most of us anywhere from twenty minutes to one or two days to recover for a second erection and orgasm.

The female orgasm is more difficult to put into words. In *Reproduction, Sex, and Preparation for Marriage,* the authors state:

> Women who have experienced an orgasm are able to describe it in physical terms only about as well as men could were there no ejaculation to describe. The female orgasm produces contractions around the rim of the vagina with perhaps some spasm of the muscles of the vagina. The uterus tilts slightly upwards. There is a general release of bodily and genital and emotional tension; she feels the need to show tenderness and warmth to her partner.

Although the experience is hard to describe, it *is* known that the woman's *capacity* for orgasm is much greater than the man's. She can experience *different intensities* of orgasm. And she doesn't require nearly the time between orgasms that men do—in fact, women have been known to have three, four, or more orgasms within the course of a few minutes.

The fact that men require substantial recovery time and women do not should make our method obvious: *Try to bring her to orgasm first.* If she climaxes before you do, then you can thrust and grind as much as you want to catch up with her. She may even enjoy a second or third orgasm while you're at it. But if *you* should ejaculate prior to her orgasm, you won't be much good for awhile. When the penis becomes limp, continued pelvic movement can be rather uncomfortable.

To eliminate the sexual guesswork, *talk to each other* during foreplay and intercourse. If her handwork has brought you to the brink of orgasm too soon, tell her (in a loving, appreciative tone) that you're just on the verge. That should be her cue to reduce the stimulation for awhile, and you should use the simmer-down time to further stimulate her. If you've already entered her, you can stave off that great moment by pausing a few seconds to lie motionless, or by adjusting your body movements so that the focus of contact is at the *base* of your penis (rubbing against the clitoris) rather than at the ultra-sensitive *head*.

She should then tell you when she feels *her* orgasm coming on, perhaps simply by saying "I'm coming ..." Those words will be music to your ears, for they are the testimony that you've done your part well.

As much as you try, however, there may be times when you just cannot help climaxing first (for obvious reasons, one's objectivity in this state tends to become rather blurred). If premature ejaculation should happen,* *never leave her frustrated by deserting her at the verge of her orgasm.* Go immediately to hand and finger stimulation of her clitoris and vagina, for she can still attain a satisfactory orgasm through your loving second effort.

THE FIFTH PHASE
Afterglow

This is the time when she needs your tender assurances the most, perhaps more than any other moment in marriage. It's

---

*If premature ejaculation has become a pronounced problem, you and your wife can conquer it through some loving, patient teamwork. As with any other sex "problem," the worst thing you can do is give up. Secure a copy of Masters and Johnson's *Human Sexual Response,* which details how a couple can work together to cure premature ejaculation, impotence, frigidity, etc. Very few sex problems are strictly organic in nature, and as a result there are even fewer problems that cannot be overcome through mutual practice and understanding.

also the time when a depressing number of husbands roll over and fall asleep. Don't minimize the importance of the afterglow, for to her it's as much a part of the love act as orgasm itself.

Hold her close as you lie together in complete, unhurried luxury. Tell her how great it felt to be *one* with her. Bathe her in soft kisses as you thank her for sharing herself with you. And keep touching and caressing her—your gentle fondling is more cherished now than ever before.

As the authors of *Reproduction, Sex, and Preparation for Marriage* state: *"This is the time when the woman draws strength, security, and serenity from the man's love for her"* (italics mine). So stay awake. Let her know that you wouldn't trade the last hour for anything else the world could offer.

So goes the mutually fulfilling sex act—the most beautiful and satisfying portrayal of married love God could have created. Of course, there will be occasions when one partner does not feel up to sexual intercourse—a perfectly normal occurrence which shouldn't be any cause for alarm. But if that partner sees that his spouse is in need of sexual release, he should have no reservations about volunteering to stimulate his spouse to singular orgasm. Neither should the spouse feel unduly selfish in receiving such stimulation, for this is what marriage is all about—*meeting the other's needs. Loving. Satisfying.*

It is not my intention that you follow the guidelines in these chapters as absolute law. That would be like asking you to keep a driver's manual in hand for constant reference as you speed down the highway.

Rather, I suggest these principles to help *free you* from any humdrum that may have invaded your married sexual experience. Utilize them to give your wife the fulfillment she deserves in this exhilarating expression of commitment and love.

21
101 Ways to Make Your Wife Feel Like That Special Woman

Is not this the true romantic feeling–not to desire to escape life, but to prevent life from escaping you?
THOMAS WOLFE

I just read about a thrifty young woman who became concerned over the lavish amount of money her boyfriend was spending on her. After an expensive dinner date, she asked her mother, "What can I do to stop Tom from spending so much money on me?"

Her mother replied simply, "Marry him."

An unfair generality? Or a perceptive comment on the state of the married male who, after a dazzling courtship and capture, turns into a dilapidated Don Juan? Why, after one year of marriage, do we often let the princely courtesies, romantic gifts, and seductive twinkles of the eye become buried by routine?

True, after you've lived with her a few years and observed some of her less-than-glamorous moments, the puppy-eyed Romeo in you is bound to give way to a more rational, less emotional foundation of love. And it should.

But woman is a romantic creature.

253

Along with that uncanny intuition and a set of brains you'd be stupid to ignore, God has made your wife with a deep craving to be loved and to be constantly *assured* of that love.

That's why the wedding should not signal the end of the courtship, but the beginning.

Much as women are enraptured by the words, "I love you," they prefer to see *expressions* of that love. The small, thoughtful gift that says, "I was thinking about you today." The candlelight dinner—with just the two of you—that tells her, "You're my favorite person in the whole world." Or just plain pitching in at home. When you volunteer to help her do any of the endless jobs that keep a house in order, she'll know that you consider her some special woman.

Kathy, like all women, is bewitched by the "little things." And since I don't need such reassurance as often as she does, I've always tended to reserve the romantic flares just for special occasions like anniversaries, birthdays, and Valentine's Day. Besides, wouldn't I go broke if I got romantic too often?

Fortunately, I wasn't long in my ignorance. One day during coffee break I was in a drugstore with a good friend, who had been married eleven years longer than I. Lowell was looking into the perfume case, his excitement mounting by the second. "Pammy *loves* this stuff," he said. "It's sure fun surprising her with it." As I watched Lowell select and purchase that bottle of perfume for his wife, I could see he was enjoying every minute of anticipation.

That set my mind to scheming. "Let's go next door to the florist," I said. It wasn't even Kathy's and my anniversary. And we hadn't had a fight in over three months. I just wanted to let her know that I loved her, cared for her, and thought she was the greatest.

As I came through the door that evening and presented the single long-stemmed rose, Kathy's squeals of delight let me know that the surprise was worth a thousand times its cost. The grateful hug and the extra-happy smile during dinner convinced me that I would forever be a romantic.

The liberated, total husband knows a good thing when he

sees one. It is the "gift" which demonstrates to his wife, his children, and the whole wide world that he is irrevocably, unapologetically in love with her. I use quotation marks here because the gift needn't always be giftwrapped—sometimes it consists of your time, your helpfulness, your willingness to listen. But the gift must always—without exception—involve a big outpouring of *you*.

I know of several smart husbands who have never stopped courting their wives. And just like mine, their marriages are filled with joyful results. When I asked them to give me some examples of little things they like to do to make their wives feel loved, I wasn't quite prepared for the deluge of ideas they gave. Along with several of my own, here are "101 Ways to Make Your Wife Feel Like That Special Woman." Use them to set your own creativity flowing.

1. Start leaving occasional love notes when you go to work. The first could be on the kitchen table or counter top. Then find some places she won't see until later in the day, like the bottom of the laundry hamper, inside the freezing compartment, etc.

2. Have her make a list of repairs or improvements that are needed around the house. Then begin doing them, one by one. You'll be amazed at how much she appreciates that new pantry shelf or a stopped leak.

3. If she's in the other room sewing, reading, or working, rush in, hug her, and give her a big kiss. "I made a special trip just to kiss you" brings a smile every time.

4. Empty the trash without her having to ask.

5. Let her know that her phone calls are *always* welcome while you're at the office. I once had a boss who never turned down a call from his wife, even during a meeting. On more than one occasion, my colleagues and I sat and listened as he closed out a conversation with an uninhibited "I love you, Honey." I respected him for it. And I'm sure his wife was proud to know that he considered her "top priority."

6. *Listen* to her when she talks to you. Look into her eyes, not at your food or the TV set. Respond *positively* whenever you can. Show her you're interested in what she has to say.

7. Phone her from work just to tell her how much you love her. Absolutely no business talk allowed. Give her the special, unexpected moment of your time, and leave the baby-sitter, the mail, the electric bill for another call.

8. Tell her, "You're my best friend." If *Joe* is really your best friend, don't fib to her. But I suggest you pursue one of two options: Leave your wife and marry Joe, or begin spending more quality time with your wife. (You'll find the second much more rewarding.)

9. Keep on making "dates" with her throughout the marriage. Ask for a date for Friday night, and tell her you'll be by at eight o'clock. Arrange for a baby-sitter. On the big night, after you've dressed, slip out of the house and come to the door for her. Then, as you walk her to the door afterwards, corner her and drop the coy old standard: "May I come in?" What follows is up to you.

10. Give her a frequent break from the dishes. No matter how tired I am after a day's work, I know that Kathy is just as pooped. She relishes the times when I tell her, "Honey, I'll do the dishes—why don't you go relax? You deserve it."

11. Write her some poetry. You don't have to be a Rod McKuen—the key is to simply express your feelings about something very intimate between the two of you. A recent walk in the woods. An argument that, when settled, helped draw you closer together. The beauty, skill, love you see in her. When a woman receives an original poem from her lover, the last thing she thinks about is literary criticism. It is from *you*—you have invested and revealed *yourself* for her. Nothing thrills a woman more.

12. Surprise her with breakfast in bed. And not just on her birthday or Mother's Day. If she asks "What's the occasion?" as you fluff her pillows behind her, just smile and say, "No particular reason.... *I just love you.*"

13. Be careful about our male habit of joking about the intelligence of women, women drivers, women talkers, women shoppers. *She's* a woman, and these baseless slurs are also a slur on her. If you have this habit, break it.

14. Give her a frequent break from the house and chil-

dren. One of my cousins is an insurance representative who has turned into a very smart husband. Every Wednesday afternoon he comes home to take care of the kids while his wife escapes for a long bike ride, an hour of shopping, a leisurely trip to the library. Getting away is a breath of fresh air to her. For him, it is time well spent with the children, and he wouldn't trade that afternoon at home for the commission from a hundred insurance policies. If you can't break away during the day, consider one evening a week, or perhaps Saturday mornings.

15. Don't run down her parents or family. Give them the benefit of a doubt, just as you'd like her to do for *your* folks.

16. Keep your own private calendar of the "special days" of your relationship and plan special surprise celebrations. Anniversaries, birthdays, Mother's Day, and Christmas are rather expected, but imagine her delight when you take the initiative to commemorate the anniversary of your first date, your engagement, your mortgage burning, etc.

17. When the kids are in school, phone her and arrange to meet during the day for lunch or an extended coffee break. Use this time to talk about your life together, plans for the family and the future, or anything that's on her mind. It will lift her spirits to see once again that, in the midst of a busy workday, you still consider her "Number One."

18. Help her keep the family correspondence going.

19. Respect her friends, and show an interest in getting to know them. If Irene drops over from next door, don't leave the room or huddle up with the television.

20. If you've given her a hamburger budget, don't complain if you don't get steak. Either allot more food money for her to work with, or begin right now appreciating the fact that she's being as creative as she knows how to be.

21. After she's spent a hard day at the stove, serve *her* during the meal. Many wives—and most mothers—are forced to eat their food cold because they are constantly hopping up from the table to serve everyone's needs. Let your woman sit and enjoy the food for once while you get another napkin for Junior or more iced tea for yourself.

And if you don't already, you might begin enforcing this family rule: Everyone (Dad included) clears his own dishes from the table.

22. To continue #21: Wash your own snack dishes.

23. Some Saturday morning—or a weekday if you can swing it—write "Let's go to the amusement park today" or "Let's go to the beach—just the two of us" on a slip of paper, stick it in a small box and giftwrap it. Present it to her with a kiss at breakfast.

24. When the two of you are at a party or gathering, catch her eye with a wink and a smile. Flirting with her in public assures her that, of all the women in that room, she's the most important to you.

25. At the same gathering, take her hand and whisper in her ear, "I can't *wait* to get you home..." She may feign embarrassment, but deep inside she'll be beaming.

26. *Never* compare her to old girl friends, your sister, Mom, or anyone else.

27. Here's a worthwhile project: When you say, "I love you," give her some specific reasons *why*. Watch her face light up as you describe the things about her that delight you.

28. Stay aware of special things she enjoys doing: going to plays, concerts, movies, picnics, etc., and take the initiative to do these things together. A smart friend of mine keeps a notebook in which he lists:

"Diane's favorite color: Blue"

"Loves ballet, roses, football"

"Has always wanted to go backpacking"

Through the years, he'll pull out one of his notations and act on it. Diane's response is an invariable "How did you know I've always wanted to do this?"

29. Keep the car serviced for her. While some of today's women are becoming viable mechanics in their own right, most are still totally helpless when the thingamabob under the whoozit goes *p-f-f-f-t-t*. And, while your wife may not mind pumping her own gas at the self-serve station, she would prefer not to when dressed in a slick pantsuit. Gas

fumes don't blend well with Chanel No. 5.

30. Make the bed in the morning while she's in the bathroom or fixing breakfast. One small task crossed off her list by a considerate husband will launch her day in higher spirits. But note: Remember what day it is. A friend of mine recently scurried around the room to make the bed while his wife was in the kitchen. As he sat down at the breakfast table, eager to see her surprise afterward, his wife said to their small son, "Jimmy, would you run and pull the sheets off all the beds? If I can hurry and get the laundry done..."

31. Pray together. Nothing will give your woman greater security than knowing that you are totally dedicated to God. Go to him together in thanks, in praise, in problem solving.

32. As you pray together, take her hand and thank God for giving her to you as a wife. If you sneak a peek (I don't think the Lord would mind), you'll probably catch her smiling.

33. Be alert to some of the small things you can do at home to help make her job easier. If you drink up the powdered milk, mix a new pitcher full. If you finish the orange juice, make a new batch. Replace the empty toilet roll. Sweep down a cobweb.

34. Feed the dog.

35. Feed the baby.

36. Change the diapers (on the baby).

37. If Junior has discovered the trick of bawling for Mommy late at night, let Mom rest. With Junior around all day, she's earned it. Tend to him yourself. Dad's firmness often has a way of convincing Junior that he really doesn't need to holler after all.

38. If company is coming and she's in a rush, offer to help in any way you can.

39. Take the initiative to wash the windows or wax the floors. Isn't it amazing how waxing the kitchen floor is tagged in our minds as strictly female work? I guess most men don't realize how hard the job really is. Some day, give it a try. Never mind what your friends may think—you are liberated from that, remember?

40. Hang up towels and clothes when you're through with them. I've managed to save Kathy a lot of extra stooping that comes when a wife has to pick up after her husband, but I'm still weak in one item of apparel: shoes. I can't stand them on my feet any longer than necessary. So when I enter the apartment, the shoes clunk to the floor—usually beside the big chair in the living room. And it's often not until I see Kathy bending over to carry my shoes to the bedroom closet that I realize that I've still got a long way to go in the sensitivity department. There just isn't a reason in this world why that beautiful woman should have to constantly clean up my own mess.

Three surprises which are like a breath of fresh air to her:

41. "Let's go out to dinner."

42. "Let's go buy you a new dress."

43. "Let's go away for the weekend—just the two of us."

44. If she's on a diet or exercise binge, *encourage her*. Fat jokes are definitely out. If you see improvement, however slight, be sure to tell her. "Honey, you're looking better and better" will bring a smile and renewed determination on her part. Incidentally, the *best* way to encourage her is to *join* her.

And while we're on encouragement:

45. Commit yourself to *building* rather than *destroying*. I know of innumerable homes and love relationships that are poisoned by the barbs of insult. The "slam" is the tool of an insecure person who will abuse the feelings of another simply to call attention to his "wit." It hurts her no matter how she may laugh. No smile, chuckle, or "just kidding, Honey" soothes the inner hurt.

Often the putdown is a husband's most creative way of striking back for a wrong his wife may have committed. It is not necessarily verbal: It can be a disdainful look, an impatient sigh which says, in effect, "I wish you were anything but what you are." Few things yank the foundations out of a marriage more quickly than the holier-than-thou spouse who makes nit-picking a way of life. Don't.

To *build* is just that—constructing a foundation of love

which will weather any future storms or quakes. A spouse committed to building recognizes that all persons come with quirks, and with that perception behind him, he looks only for the good in others. He is quick to compliment, slow to complain. Do.

To the husband who feels these paragraphs may be directed to the wrong half of the marriage, a hint worth remembering: The act of building another is steadily contagious. If your wife is the culprit when it comes to tearing into another, do not retaliate. That is the most natural approach, but also the weakest. Respond with something positive. Smile. Build. As you direct attention to the admirable qualities in your woman, she will try even harder to be all you're saying she is. And gradually, she will catch on to how enjoyable it is to build in return.

46. Leave the toilet seat *down* when you're through with it.

47. Consider taking on hobbies, sports, etc., that include her and the children. While an escape valve is important for today's eight-to-five male, that workshop or golf course can easily become an obsession in itself, and thus a barrier to time and talk with family. But it needn't be. Some of the closest times I had with my family while growing up were times of recreation. Dad always knew the value of a family camp-out, or of teaching his sons how to build birdhouses, doghouses, or soapbox racers in the workshop.

48. If you're the sanguine of the family, you might help to draw her out in discussions. When we're with friends, I have the tendency to dominate the Benson side of the conversation, not even allowing for Kathy's input on a subject. She thinks awhile before saying something. I often talk before thinking. But I can tell she gets a good feeling inside when I ask her to share her views. "What do *you* think, Honey?" is the demonstration that I consider her opinion important.

49. Tell your children often how much you love their mother. Then let them see it in action every day. If you treat her like a queen, they'll want to, too.

50. Scheme with the kids on creative ways to surprise

Mom—breakfast in bed, cleaning the house when she's gone, a special gift, dinner out. Let them make the presentation. It's good family fun, and she'll be proud of the fatherly talents you're displaying.

51. Take the phone off the hook before and during dinner. At our house, dinnertime is family time, and woe be to the salesman who interrupts with a crude appeal over the phone lines.

52. Never let holding her hand become past tense. It's one of those little things which a woman never grows tired of. In sitting or walking together, seek out her hand and give it a little squeeze.

53. *Exception:* Avoid the above when she's drying her nail polish. Your affections won't be duly appreciated.

54. If you like her outfit, tell her *"You* make it look good."

55. If you *don't* like her outfit or hairstyle, she really wants to know it. She wants to please you. But even here the total man is more tactful than, "What happened to your hair—did you grab an electrified fence?"

I love the way Kathy wears her hair—long and full, surrounding her face in cute flips. But occasionally, when the weather gets hot, she'll draw it back tight and stack it on top of her head. Not exactly the way I prefer it. One day, she must have noticed. "Do you like me with my hair up?" she asked.

Though she didn't intend it, she had asked a trick question, and I had to think fast. "Yes, Honey, I like *you* even if you go bald," I assured her. The hairstyle, like it or not, has nothing to do with my love for *her.*

Assurances accomplished, I still needed to provide a good answer to her question. I think I found one. "Honey," I said, "I'll give you an honest opinion: I think you've got a beautiful face. And *gorgeous* hair to frame it. I think God made them to complement each other, just like a frame enhances a painting." Being an artist herself, Kathy got my meaning.

You may sometimes find it difficult to wax poetic as I managed to, but here's a principle that deserves attention: When commenting on an "undesirable" outfit or hairstyle, make a clear distinction between your feelings for the outfit and your feelings for her. Compliment *her* in the process. Example: "Honey, you've got such a sexy body (or face) that this baggy pantsuit (or stringy hairdo) just doesn't do you justice."

56. Keep surprising her with the little things that can mean so much:

A flower (bring one home with you)
A bouquet (have the florist deliver it to her during the day)
A plant
A scented candle
A slinky nightgown (shopping for it is half the fun)
An album by her favorite performer or group
A book she's been wanting to read
Perfume
A romantic or humorous card
A craft which you, she, and the kids can work on together
A ring or necklace

57. Better yet, surprise her with something you've made yourself:

Woodwork
Sculpture
A painting
A card (with original poetry and/or original art)
Candles

Because you have put yourself into it, the husband-made gift is priceless to her. Long after she has thrown away the perfume bottle, the store-bought greeting card, or the wilted flower, she will be keeping your hand-made gift as a priceless treasure.

58. Accompany a surprise gift with "... because I love you." Not with "Because I want to get it on with you in bed tonight" or even "Because you did such-and-such for me."

Just "... because I love you." Love expects absolutely nothing in return.

59. And while we're on gifts: When it comes to Christmas, birthdays, and anniversaries, most women think a little differently than we do. While I'd be delighted to get an electric drill, Kathy would have trouble rejoicing over an electric frying pan. Why? Because it's *practical*. Like when you receive socks for your birthday. Six or seven pair of them. Skinny black ones.

Now an electric frying pan is fine, and so are skinny black socks. What I'm saying is that the special occasions are meant to give her a *break* from the routine, not a reminder of it. Use these times of the year to sniff out the creative little extravagances that tell her she's well worth a splurge.

60. Phone her when you're delayed in coming home from work.

61. Phone her well in advance of inviting a friend home to dinner. And *ask* her; don't *tell* her.

62. Use the phone often when taking a business trip. Even the strongest woman is asking these questions while you're away:

Is he safe?
Is he being faithful?
Is he staying in good health?
Does he miss me?

I know some smart husbands who call their wives every night when they're traveling. Not out of any henpecked obligation, but out of a love which wants to assure their wives that they can't wait to get back. It makes for healthier wives and happier homes. Some companies, in fact, are beginning to reimburse their businessmen for long-distance calls between husband and wife. Evidently they look on this closer communication as a good investment.

63. Save her an ounce of undue worry—if she's gone on an errand and you have to leave the house yourself, leave a note for her with your destination and the approximate

amount of time you'll be gone.

64. Appreciate her—inwardly *and* verbally. One wife told me how she was so thrilled early in her marriage when her husband said to her—in front of his mother, no less— "Honey, your cherry pies are just fantastic."

65. Do you give yourself a personal spending allowance every payday? Fine. Now what about her? Give her an allowance equal to yours, to do with as she chooses. This has some decided advantages:

It demonstrates that you take the partnership concept seriously.

It helps her to have a certain degree of independence within a happy marriage.

It helps both of you to stay within the budget by having a specific allotment for free spending.

66. For all the reasons listed above, consider opening a separate savings and/or checking account for her, in which she can deposit or withdraw money *she* earns. Surprise her with the news. Tell her the account(s) are hers to manage as she pleases (her prudence just might surprise you).

67. If a fixture in your house is in need of repair, don't make her struggle with it for days. Fix it right away.

68. When you come home from the office, search her out and give her a big, prolonged hug. First thing. Before sitting down with the paper or using the john. Make your wife feel that coming home to her has been the best part of your day.

69. Set aside a few minutes, a half-hour, or more each day just to visit with her. Make it a time when the kids are busy or in bed, when the dishes are done and she's had a while to relax. After you've taken the phone off the hook, talk together about the things on each other's minds ... about goals ... about dreams.

I know some very successful parents of six children who long ago placed a sofa along the wall in their bedroom. There, almost every evening when the children had been tucked away for the night, they would sit, hold hands, and visit together privately. Now the children are almost all married, some with children of their own. But their parents are still holding their regular evening rendezvous on that sofa. Theirs is one of the best marriages I have known in my life.

Don't let even house guests pull you away from this time together. An extended stay by Jack and Harriet is when your woman may need to be alone with you the most.

70. Find a pet name that she likes—one that expresses love and high regard for her.

71. Praise her. *Tell others* what you appreciate about your wife. Whenever I read Proverbs 31, about the virtuous woman, I can see one big reason why she did so well—have you ever noticed what her husband did? "He praises her in the gates," where the elders of the city met to transact business. And her children? "They rise up to call her blessed." With that kind of encouragement, no wonder she was such a motivated, successful woman!

72. True, home is to be lived in. But as a perpetual slob? Your continual lolling around in a pock-marked T-shirt and 1961 Bermudas is about as exciting to her as hair rollers are to you. Pay some attention to your appearance just as you did while you were dating her.

73. Accompany her when she goes grocery shopping, especially if she must go at night.

74. Don't be threatened by the idea of shopping with her for women's clothing or fabric. Be interested in items which appeal to her. Give her your honest opinion when she points to something (but review #55!).

It's amazing how modern acculturation has molded men's minds in this area, too. One day I sat down in our local shopping mall, in a spot where I could watch the doorways of several shops. Within just a few minutes I counted twelve couples entering a popular women's clothing store. Seven of the twelve men hesitated before finally entering with an embarrassed, "Ah, gee..." expression on their faces. A few of them stood and waited for their wives just inside the doorway. Several single women entered, then along came a thirteenth couple. The male half of this duo couldn't even bring it upon himself to go in. He stood outside the entrance, sputtering like an impatient child while his woman surveyed the shop.

Chalk up some more members for the Archie Bunker society.

75. Try to be consistent in expressing appreciation for her work in the house. When you come home, notice the rooms that are straightened and vacuumed, your ironed shirts, the aroma of what's cooking. Compliment and thank her as you give her a warm hug.

Three statements she'll never grow tired of hearing:

76. "You're beautiful today."

77. "I'm glad you're my wife."

78. "You're my favorite person."

79. Over the phone, in a letter, or in person, tell her folks how much you love their daughter. You can bet that the word will get around to her.

80. *Always* put time with her and the children before time with the TV set.

81. Put the paper or book down when she tries to talk to you.

82. Do your part of the job of disciplining the kids. Though it is the father who should take the lead here, far too many men have relegated discipline to the mother. This is not to say that Mom can't handle the job; but when she is the only one wielding the stick, Dad comes across to Junior as a nonassertive pantywaist. You can bet that Junior will grow up to be the same. Enforce the rules of the house in love but in firmness. Remember the wise words of Solomon: "If you refuse to discipline your son, it proves that you don't love him; for if you love him you will be prompt to punish him" (Proverbs 13:24, TLB).

83. Support her in the discipline she *must* do. If she has made a disciplinary decision while you're away, don't contradict her when you come home. The same should apply to

her. Incidentally, the children should be taught that Mom and Dad always support each others' decisions or disciplinary measures. Never let children play one of you against the other in trying to win a favorable verdict.

Watch for the smile in her eyes when you dust off some of those "manners" which supposedly went out of date a decade ago:

84. Open her car door for her (even if she'll be doing the driving).

85. Help seat her at the dinner table.

86. After you've seated her, give her a kiss on the cheek and whisper "I love you." (When the kids see these things happen, their respect for Mom will zoom. Your ratings won't hurt any, either.)

87. Open doors for her, letting her enter first. (Next time you're in town, watch a while—this is becoming a lost art.)

88. When walking with her, walk on the most hazardous side. This used to always be the street side of the walk, but with today's modern curbs and protective rails, no definite Amy Vanderbilt can be stated. In many cities, the shadows and lurkways on the *in*side of the walk pose more potential threat than the most reckless car.

89. A few years ago I read about this gift idea, and decided to put it to work on Valentine's Day:

At the local drugstore, I asked the pharmacist for a box of empty gelatin capsules. After eyeing me suspiciously, he asked, "What are you using them for?"

"For a gift for my wife," I said. The guy just stood there "To put little notes in," I hastened to add, "and she'll open one each week for the next year."

He still said nothing, but his expression said, *"Su-u-r-r-e."* After another long moment (during which I was convinced he would call out the narcotics squad) he brought me the capsules.

Back in my office, I counted out fifty-two capsules and slipped a sheet of paper into the typewriter. Within half an hour I had typed out fifty-two one-liners such as:

"One movie of your choice with hubby"
"Two nights' freedom from dishwashing"
"One pizza on the evening of your choice"
"One good, long walk together"
"One long, leisurely breakfast out together"
"One trip to the beach together"
"One new outfit of your choice"
"One new nightgown (of *my* choice)"

Some involve spending some money, others merely time—but each involves *togetherness*. I took a pair of scissors to the sheet, then rolled up each note and inserted one in each capsule.

When Kathy opened the little package, the prescription on the little bottle read, "RX from Dr. Dan Benson for Kathy Benson: To prevent dull marriage, take one capsule every week for the next year."

The gift meant many fun times together. Half the fun was watching Kathy continually fight off the urge to open them all at once.

90. A variation on the above: When the mood strikes, set a "loaded" pill out in the morning with the rest of her vitamins. (You'd better be there to be sure it doesn't go down with the Vitamin C.) Let her claim the activity or gift during the day.

91. Never speak negatively of her to another person—in her presence or in her absence. Anything undesirable in the woman you love is strictly between you and her—and should be worked out in loving, honest communication with each other.

Exercise these nine qualities of total manhood with her:

92. *Love* ... always seeking the best for her. Realizing that the opposite of love is not hate, but *self.*

93. *Joy* ... a happiness so deeply rooted that it is not swayed by the whims of circumstance. Rejoicing in victory. Optimistic in adversity.

94. *Peace* ... a quiet assurance, in spite of circumstances, that the One who loves both of you is also seeking the *best* for you. Looking on problems as opportunities.

THE TOTAL MAN

95. *Patience* ... always giving her the benefit of the doubt. Putting yourself in her place. Looking beyond the *what* to learn the *why*.

96. *Kindness* ... giving of yourself simply to bring joy to her. Watching for ways to make her load lighter.

97. *Goodness* ... creating an atmosphere in which evil is conspicuously out of place. The foundational attitude from which acts of kindness flow.

98. *Faithfulness* ... fidelity in body, mind, and spirit, motivated by an irrevocable, unconditional love for her.

99. *Gentleness* ... being confident enough in masculinity to know that caring, communicating, expressing emotion, or playing with the children do not contradict manhood, but enhance it.

100. *Self-control* ... not allowing any activity or appetite to displace God and her in your affections. Recognizing that your temperance in diet, spending, work, and play affects *her* as much as yourself.

101. Realize that no man can exercise these nine qualities of total manhood on his own strength—for in his natural state he is prone to selfishness. As stated earlier, the apostle Paul identified this source of manhood when he called these nine attributes "the fruit of the Spirit." He was speaking of God's Spirit, from which all goodness, all dynamism flows. It is only by the daily putting of your life into *God's* hands that love, joy, peace, patience, kindness, goodness, faithfulness, gentleness, and self-control become a natural outgrowth of a pure inner man.

God, then, is the daily motivator for all attributes and outflows of total manhood. And the husband's solid walk with God will be his wife's greatest source of security.

RESORUCES

Chapter 1 "Why Men Won't Seek Help," James Lincoln Collier, *The Reader's Digest,* September, 1975.
"Culture and Coronaries," *Time,* August 18, 1975.

Chapter 2 *The Changing Success Ethic,* an AMA Survey Report, Dale Tarnowski, 1973.

Chapter 3 "The Search for a New American Dream," John Peterson, *The National Observer,* January 10, 1976.

Chapter 4 *Managing Your Time,* Ted Engstrom and Alec MacKenzie; Zondervan, 1968.
"How to Make the Most of Your Time," Interview with R. Alec MacKenzie, *U. S. News and World Report,* December 3, 1973.
"Type A Behavior Indicted Again," *The Reader's Digest,* February, 1976.

Chapter 5 *You Can Do It!,* William Proxmire; Simon and Schuster, 1973.
The New Aerobics, Kenneth Cooper; M. Evans Company, 1970.
Total Fitness, Laurence E. Morehouse and Leonard Gross; Simon and Schuster, 1975.
Dr. Atkins' Diet Revolution, Robert C. Atkins; McKay, 1972.
"Neurosis? No, Caffeine," *The Reader's Digest,* March 1975.

Chapter 6 *Royal Canadian Air Force Exercise Plans for Physical Fitness,* Pocket Books; Simon and Schuster, 1972.

The Problem-Oriented Practice, Methodist Hospital, Inc., Indianapolis, 1976.
"25 New Tips to Help You Lose Weight," Jean Nidetch, *National Enquirer,* December 9, 1975.
Diet Tips and Tricks, Dell Purse Book; Dell Publishing Company, 1975.
Sleeping Without Pills, Mangalore N. Pai, Dell Purse Book; Dell Publishing Company, 1974.

Chapter 7   "Death of a Tycoon," *Time,* March, 1975.

Chapter 9   "People," *Worldwide Challenge,* Campus Crusade for Christ International, 1975.

Chapter 11   *How to Get Control of Your Time and Your Life,* Alan Lakein; The New American Library, 1973.

Chapter 14   "A Good Spat ... Best Thing for Your Marriage," Gary Stemm, *National Enquirer,* December 22, 1975.

Chapter 15   *Cherishable: Love and Marriage,* David W. Augsburger; Herald Press, 1971.
"Checklist for Fathers," John M. Drescher, *Eternity,* October, 1972.
"Fathers Wanted!" Paul Popenoe, source unknown.
Hide or Seek, James Dobson; Fleming H. Revell, 1974.
Between Parent and Child, Haim Ginott; The Macmillan Company, 1965.

Chapters   *How to Succeed with Your Money,* George M.
16 & 17   Bowman; Moody Press, 1974.
Sylvia Porter's Money Book, Sylvia Porter; Doubleday, 1975.
"Are You Over Your Head in Debt?" *Better Homes and Gardens,* June, 1975.
"Why Some People Spend Too Much," *Women's Day,* June, 1974.
"Managing the Money Squeeze," Norman Lobsenz, *Reader's Digest,* February, 1976.

Chapters   *The Joy of Sex,* Alex Comfort; Crown Publishers,
18, 19 & 20   1972.
"Sex Problems and Sex Techniques in Marriage," Ed Wheat (tape album)
Reproduction, Sex and Marriage, Lawrence Q. Crawley, James L. Malfetti, Ernest I. Stewart, Nini Vas Dias; Prentice-Hall, 1964.